MARC H. ELLIS

The Renewal of Palestine In The Jewish Imagination

WIPF & STOCK · Eugene, Oregon

Wipf and Stock Publishers
199 W 8th Ave, Suite 3
Eugene, OR 97401

The Renewal of Palestine In the Jewish Imagination
By Ellis, Marc H.
Copyright©1994 by Ellis, Marc H.
ISBN 13: 978-1-4982-9655-7
Publication date 5/2/2016
Previously published by Alhani International Books Ltd., 1994

TO ROSEMARY RADFORD RUETHER
AND
HERC RUETHER
WHOSE FRIENDSHIP AND SOLIDARITY
HAVE HELPED SUSTAIN ME.

contents

Preface **7**

Chapter One

   I Israel and the future of the Jewish people **11**
   II The limitation of Holocaust theology **17**
   III The occupation is over **27**
   IV A new theological framework **35**

Chapter Two

   I Beyond the Jewish-Christian dialogue:
     Solidarity with the Palestinian people **45**
   II Jewish progressives and the Palestinians **49**
   III Solidarity with the Palestinians **57**

IV Christian theology and the Palestinian
   uprising **67**
V Toward a Jewish-Christian Palestinian
   solidarity **85**

Chapter Three

   I The renewal of Palestine in the Jewish
     imagination **91**
  II An inclusive liturgy of destruction **95**
 III The failure of Jewish theology **107**
  IV Palestine before Israel: A dangerous
     memory **119**
   V Palestine and the Jewish future **137**
  IV Ending Auschwitz **147**

Afterword

Next year in Jerusalem **153**

PREFACE

I am very pleased that these essays are being published for the first time in the United Kingdom, as they represent both a continuity and an evolution of my journey over the past decade. Each essay responds to or initiates what became, without prior planning, a trilogy of books on the subject of Jewish theology in relation to the ongoing crisis in Israel and Palestine: *Toward a Jewish Theology of Liberation (1987), Beyond Innocence and Redemption: Confronting the Holocaust and Israeli Power (1990), and Ending Auschwitz: Reflections on the Future of Jewish and Christian Life* (1994). I have also included an Afterword that concerns the newest political developments in the Middle East, specifically the accord reached between Israel and the Palestine Liberation Organization in September 1993.

Beyond the immediate issues of politics and economics lie the larger and deeper realities of history and fidelity. As a Jew I am asking in these essays traditional religious questions in light of our present circumstances : What does it mean to be Jewish after the Holocaust and the consolidation of our empowerment in Israel/Palestine? Coming from a situation of oppression, what does it mean for Jewish history and theology to continue oppressing the Palestinian people? Has our empowerment in Israel brought us the freedom we so urgently needed, or has our abuse of power in Israel brought us a new enslavement and ghettoisation which we did not seek, but now pursue almost blindly? Can we be healed of our trauma of Holocaust by finalising the trauma of the Palestinian people which we as Jews have inflicted? At the lighting of the Shabbat candles, shall we bless our endeavour and thank God for making us into a warrior people?

I do not pretend to answer all these questions in the essays presented here, nor maintain that the essays represent a coherent platform for immediate political action to address the Middle East crisis. Rather they represent a plea to create a framework of healing of Jew and Palestinian before it is too late. The current talk of autonomy, limited self-rule, or even the withdrawal from Gaza and Jericho, which for many seems hopeful is, at least to my mind, a pursuit of the end of Palestine through negotiation. From the Jewish side, autonomy as it is being presented is a plan of ghettoisation and division of Palestinians and Palestine. As Jews, we seem unable to see that the "peace process" is less a setting of political intrigue than it is a referendum on Jewish history. It will determine who we as a Jewish people become and the legacy we bequeath to our children. In light of the suffering which we lived through, do we now want to pass on to our children a legacy of displacing, expropriating, torturing and murdering others?

Despite the rhetoric to the contrary, the end of a viable Palestine, and therefore the end of an ethically based Jewish life, is near. Yet until the final moment, history is open. There is still time if we seize the moment. This at least is my understanding of the fidelity which is a necessary response to the drama of Jewish and Palestinian history at the close of the twentieth century.

CHAPTER ONE

Israel and the future of the Jewish people

With the decisive victory of Israel in the June 1967 Six Day War, certain trends in Jewish theological understanding crystallised. It might be said that the war itself posed both sides of a dialectic present in Jewish life since the discovery of the death camps and the emergence of the state of Israel: the dialectic of Holocaust and empowerment. Because of the perpetual diaspora situation over the last two thousand years and the difficulty of humanly absorbing the Nazi attempt to impose a "final solution" to the Jewish question, theological responses to this new dialectic were naturally slow in coming. A revolution in theological thought was needed to match the revolutionary change in the Jewish condition, i.e., the loss of European Jewry, the shift of diaspora Jewish power to North America, and the reality of a Jewish state. After the Six Day War, the philosophical transformation was solidified and articulated by Holocaust theologians who, in despair and courage, charted a theology that is now normative for the Jewish community throughout the world.[1]

In its beginnings Holocaust theology, as pioneered by Elie Wiesel, Emi Fackenheim, Richard Rubenstein, and Irving Greenberg, was radical, incisive, and controversial. It spoke about and named the collective trauma the Jewish people had experienced as a, or often as *the*, formative event of Jewish history. Holocaust theologians juxtaposed the Holocaust with the biblical origins of the Jewish community to pose the question of God's fidelity to a covenanted people. They challenged the Rabbinic tradition both in its theological analysis of the diaspora condition and the type of leadership, or lack thereof, it provided in the moment of greatest adversity. At the same, time Holocaust theologians critically analysed the dark side of modernity with its landscape of mass dislocation and mass death.[2]

1- For an extended analysis of the themes in Holocuast see Marc H. Ellis, *Toward a Jewish Theology of Liberation: The Uprising and the Future*. (Maryknoll, NY; Orbis, 1989) 7-24.

2- For an early radical and controversial analysis of these themes see Richard L. Rubenstein, *After Auschwitz: Radical Theology and Contemporary Judaism* (New York: Bobbs-Merrill, 1966) and *The Coming of History: Mass Death and the American Future* (New York: Harper and Row, 1975).

While the formative event of the Holocaust encouraged retrospective probing of traditional Jewish understandings in the theological and political realms, it demanded even more urgently the development of a framework for sustaining Jewish survival in the present. For if Holocaust theologians understood anything with great clarity, it was that the Holocaust was the most disorienting event in Jewish history. Thus in the midst of broken lives and shattered faiths, Holocaust theologians needed to articulate a future for the Jewish people.[3]

The genius of the Holocaust theologians was that they understood that the prospective search needed to be as radical as their retrospective probings. And that somehow within the radical questioning of past and future, the Jewish people would need a sustaining faith, one no longer overtly theological. Hence, in order to survive in the face of a disorienting event, a redefinition of what it meant to be Jewish was the task before this emerging theology. Defining a practising Jew as one who engaged in study, ritual, and observance of the law was no longer adequate, and Holocaust theologians knew it. They also understood that religious

---

3- Of course, the first priority was to survive as a people so that a future was possible to imagine. This question of survival was described by Emil Fackenheim as the commanding voice of Auchswitz. See Emil Fackenheim, *God's Presence in History: Jewish Affirmation and Philosophical Reflections* (New York: New York University Press, 1970).

affiliation or nonaffiliation would be an insufficient test of fidelity to the Jewish people. What they offered instead was a framework to integrate diverse experiences and outlooks into a strong solidarity with the future of the Jewish people. No longer would the primary commitment to synagogue, to liberal/radical politics, or to an assimilationist indifference suffice. What was needed was a broad and energetic commitment to the commands of the Holocaust experience: memory, survival, and empowerment, especially as embodied in the state of Israel. It was these commands that allowed for the continuation of the people so that at some point in history there would be a context for the resolution of the questions posed by the Holocaust. In a sense, Holocaust theologians gathered the Jewish people together for the only kind of Sinai experience possible after the Holocaust.[4]

The task of charting the future of the Jewish people was even more complex than its internal community components. The new Sinai, in gathering Jews of different persuasions into a transformed covenant, demanded a radical probing of the diverse words Jews lived within, including the

---

4- For an interesting exploration of this new framework see Irving Greenberg, "Cloud of Smoke, Pillar of Fire: Judaism, Christianity and Modernity After the Holocaust," in *Auschwitz: Beginning of a New Era?* ed. Eva Fleischner (New York: KTAV, 1977), 7-55, and "On the Third Èra of Jewish History: Power and Politics," in *Perspectives* (New York: National Jewish Resource Center, 1980).

worlds of Christianity and modernity. Indictment of historical Christianity was simple enough, at least in its overt institutional capacity; apathy toward, complicity in, and solidarity with the murderers was the order of the day. The "righteous gentiles" were clearly a minority to be mentioned, though often in passing and surely as exceptions. The collapse of European culture and values, the need to emphasise the dark side of the ideology of progress, the failure of the democracies to respond to massive Jewish refuge populations - these were more difficult issues to face. Modernity, as a promise to the world of human betterment and freedom, and especially emancipation for the Jewish people, needed a radical analysis as well. Thus Holocaust theologians confronted a dual crisis of massive proportions involving the shattering of the Jewish people and the failure of modernity.

Just as they responded to the crisis of Jewish life by creating a framework for solidarity among the Jewish people, Holocaust theologians responded to the crisis of modernity by envisioning a solidarity for those consigned to the other side of a century of progress. Richard Rubenstein and Irving Greenberg have crystallised this struggle to articulate a theological thesis for our time. "The passage of time has made it increasingly evident that a hitherto unbreachable moral and political barrier in the history of Western civilisation was successfully overcome by the Nazis in World War II and that henceforth the systematic, bureaucratic administered extermination of millions of citizens or subject peoples will forever be one of the capacities and temptations of government." They explain further that the "victims ask us, above all, not to allow the creation of another matrix of values that might sustain another attempt at genocide." The terrible tragedy of the Holocaust thus lay in the future as much as in the past.[5]

5- Rubenstein, *Cunning of History*, 28; Greenberg, "Cloud of Smoke," 29.

The limitations of Holocaust theology

By 1975, just eight years after the conclusion of the Six Day War, Holocaust theologians had addressed the crisis of the Jewish people and modernity, proposed a framework for solidarity among the Jewish people and others suffering around the world, and thus had outlined the essential dimensions of Holocaust theology as we inherit it today. Holocaust theologians succeeded in the task that faces all theology : to nurture the questions that allow us to understand the history we are participating in and creating. Yet it was at this moment, the time when Holocaust theology became normative for the Jewish people, that its critical edge became elusive. Holocaust theology was succumbing to that to which all theologies inevitably succumb: it no longer addressed the questions critical to the history the Jewish people were creating. The reasons for this failure are complex and beyond the scope of

The renewal of Palestine in the Jewish imagination

this essay. Suffice it to say here that Holocaust theology emerged out of a situation of powerlessness that demanded a mobilisation of psychic energy and material activity toward empowerment. The dialect of Holocaust and empowerment acted as a counterbalance and a critique of weakness and empire. However it did not have within it a way of analysing power once it had been achieved. Because of the experience of Holocaust, the theology lacked objectivity regarding power in Jewish hands and thus could not address the cost of our empowerment.[6]

In fact as the situation in Israel changed over time, with expanded borders, two decades of occupation, the invasion of Lebanon, and an increasing role in global arms sales and foreign policy intrigue, Holocaust theology's dialectic remained as it had crystallised at the moment of the 1967 triumph. What did change was its emphasis on empowerment. The critical role of the Holocaust diminished. We might say that in this process the Holocaust became the servant of power, called upon to legitimate activity that hitherto was seen as unethical, even immoral. Jews in the United States were in the most difficult situation of all diaspora communities: maintaining a highly visible support of Israel and creating the climate for an expanded U.S.

---

6. For an extended discussion of Holocaust theology's inability to analyse the case of empowerment see Ellis, *Jewish Theology of Liberation*, 25-37.

role in support of that state as necessary for its survival, while being relatively powerless to affect Israeli domestic and foreign policy even when in profound disagreement with it.[7]

As Holocaust theology lost its ability to enter critically into the contemporary situation of the Jewish people, its reliance on empowerment became more and more obvious. A strange paradox ensued that continues today: a theology that poses the most radical religious and ethical questions functions politically in a neo-conservative manner. Not only are the most articulate Holocaust theologians neo-conservative in their political stances, they help to legitimate the shift of Jewish intellectuals from the left to the centre and right of centre on the political spectrum. Even Holocaust theologians with previous liberal credentials bear analysis. By the 1980's Irving Greenberg, who wrote so eloquently about the prophetic call of the victims of the Holocaust in the 1970's, was essentially supporting the reemergence of American power under Ronald Reagan. At the same time, he warned against the misuse of the prophetic to undermine the security of the state of

---

7. In effect, a new pragmatism is stressed that allows the "occasional use of immoral strategies to achieve moral ends." With this understanding, the memory of the Holocaust enables Israel to be a "responsible and restrained conqueror." See Irving Greenberg, "The Third Great Cycle in Jewish History." in *Perspectives* (New York: National Jewish Resource Center, 1981), 25, 26. The recent uprising in the occupied territories and the response of Israeli authorities exemplify the difficult position diaspora Jews are in relative to Israel.

Israel: "There is a danger that those who have not grasped the full significance of the shift in the Jewish condition will judge Israel by the ideal standards of the state of powerlessness, thereby not only misjudging but unintentionally collaborating with attempted genocide." The subliminal if not overt message is clear : those who dissent carry a heavy burden to the point of creating the context for another holocaust.[8]

However, because of the Palestinian uprising, increasing numbers of Jews are beginning to understand that our historical situation has changed radically in the last two decades and that something terrible, almost tragic, is happening to us. With what words do we speak such anguished sentiments? Do we feel alone with these feelings so that they are better left unspoken? Do such words, once spoken, condemn us as traitors or with the epithet, self-hating Jew? Or does articulating the unspeakable challenge the community to break through the silence and paralysis that threatens to engulf us? And those of us who know and empathise with the Palestinians, can we speak without being accused of creating a context for another holocaust? Can we be seen as emissaries of an option to halt the cycle of destruction and death?[9]

8- Ibid, 25. Also see ibid, "Third Era," 6, and ibid, "Power and Peace," *Perspectives* 1 (December 1985): 3, 5.

9- One such attempt to break through the silence is found in David Grossman, *The Yellow Wind*, trans. Haim Watzman (New York:: Farrar, Straus and Giroux, 1988).

This is the challenge that faces the Jewish people. And with it lies the task of creating a new Jewish theology consonant with the history we are creating and the history we want to bequeath to our children. When all is said and done, should it be that we are powerful where once we were weak, that we are invincible where once we were vulnerable? Or would we rather be able to say that the power we created, necessary and flawed, was simply a tool to move beyond empowerment to a liberation that encompassed those struggling for justice, including those we once knew as enemy? And that our power, used in solidarity with others, brought forth a healing in the world that ultimately began to heal us of our wounds from over the millennia?

New movements of renewal within the Jewish community that have developed or expanded during the uprising point the way to this theology. In Israel, the Committee Confronting the Iron Fist, made up of Israelis and Palestinians, whose first publication carried the provocative title "We Will Be Free In Our Own Homeland," creates dialogue situations and stages demonstrations to end the occupation. Members of the anti-war movement Yesh Gvul, or There Is A Limit, made up of Israelis who refused to serve in the Lebanese war and today refuse to serve in the West Bank and Gaza, are courageous in their willingness to say "no" to the oppression of others, even at the expense of imprisonment. Women in

Black, made up of Israelis who hold vigils in mourning dress, and Women Against Occupation, who adopt Palestinian political prisoners and detainees, are just two more of many Jewish groups protesting the occupation and expressing solidarity with the Palestinian uprising.[10]

Since the uprising, North American Jews are increasingly vocal about justice in the Middle East. New Jewish Agenda, a movement of secular and religious Jews, continues to argue for Israeli security and the just demands of Palestinian nationhood. *Tikkun*, the progressive Jewish magazine, is in the forefront of vocal argument and organising for a new understanding of the Israeli-Palestinian situation. And now with the recent crisis, Jewish intellectuals such as Arthur Hertzberg and Irving Howe, and institutions, including the Union of American Hebrew Congregations, have voiced their horror at Israeli policies in the occupied territories.[11]

10- For the first publication of the Committee Confronting the Iron Fist see *We Will be Free in Our Own Homeland: A Collection of Readings for International Day of Fast and Solidarity with Palestinian Prisoners* (Jerusalem: Committee Confronting the Iron Fist, 1986). A report on Yesh Gvul can be found in "Israeli Doves Arousing Little Response," *New York Times*, 1 March 1988. Also see "A Captians Ideals Lead Him to Jail," *New York Times* 20 March 1988.

11- For New Jewish Agenda's response to the uprising see Ezra Goldstein and Deena Hurwitz, "No Status Quo Ante," *New Jewish Agenda* 24 (Spring 1988): 1-3. Also see Arthur Hertzberg's "The Uprising," *New York Review of Books*, 4 February 1988, 30-32; and "The Illusion of Jewish Unity" *New York Review of Books* 16 June 1988, 6, 8, 10, 11, 12. For a more personal account see Albert Vorspan, "Soul Searching," *New York Times Magazine*, 8 May 1988, 40, 41, 51, 54.

What these individuals and movements represent is a groping toward a theological framework that nurtures rather than hinders expressions of solidarity. It is almost as if a long repressed unease is coming to the surface, breaking through the language and symbol once deemed appropriate. Of course, the risk is that if the crisis passes without fundamental change, the language of solidarity will recede and the more familiar patterns will reassert themselves. And it is true that even the movements cited are often limited in their scope and vision, equivocating where necessary to retain some credibility within the Jewish community still dominated by the framework of Holocaust theology.

Still the drift is unmistakable and the task clear. The theological framework we need to create is hardly a departure, but a renewal of the themes that lie at the heart of our tradition, the exodus and the prophetic, interpreted in the contemporary world. A Jewish theology of liberation is our oldest theology, our great gift to the world, that has atrophied time and again only to be rediscovered by our own community and other communities around the world. A Jewish theology of liberation confronts Holocaust and empowerment with the dynamic of solidarity, providing a bridge to others as it critiques our own abuses of power. By linking us to all those who struggle for justice, a Jewish theology of liberation will, in the long run, decrease our sense of isolation and abandonment and thus begin a process of healing so necessary to the future of the Jewish community.

If it is true that we cannot go back behind empowerment, we now know that we cannot go forward alone. Could it be that the Palestinian faces that now confront us somehow reflect on the future of the Jewish people? This is why partial withdrawal from the occupied territories, offers of limited self-rule, autonomy, or even a two-state solution is only the beginning of a long and involved process that demands political compromise and a theological transformation that is difficult to envision. For if our theology is not confronted and transformed, then the political solutions will be superficial and transitory. A political solution may give impetus to this theological task; a theological movement may nurture a political solution. However, a political solution without a theological transformation simply enshrines the tragedy to be repeated.

Here we enter the most difficult of areas. The presupposition that in the faces of the Palestinians lies the future of what it means to be Jewish, that at the centre of the struggle to be faithful as a Jew today is the suffering and liberation of the Palestinian people, is hardly considered in Jewish theological circles - despite the uprising. At some point, though, an essential integration of Jew and Palestinian in a larger area of political, cultural, and religious life is integral to a Jewish future. However, this assumes that a fundamental confession and repentance of past and present transgressions is possible and a critical understanding of our history developed.

The occupation is over

Since the beginning of the uprising, we have awakened to reports of the torture and death of Palestinian people, mostly youths, in the occupied territories. This raises a strange and disturbing question: if Palestinians cease to die, will the uprising - at least for North American Jews and Christians - cease to matter? A horrible thought follows: for the Palestinian cause, it is crucial that they continue to die in ever increasing numbers to drive home the understanding that the occupation, as we have known it, is over. Unable to accept this conclusion, I approached a Palestinian acquaintance and a Christian who had just returned from the West Bank; both had the same thought. The Palestinian leadership - as well as the Palestinian villagers - understand the tragic fact that the uprising is dependent on the continuing torture and death of Palestinian youth.

The renewal of Palestine in the Jewish imagination

Can Jewish Israelis continue to torture and kill Palestinian youth *ad infinitum*? Can North American Jews continue to support these horrible acts? And can Christians, especially those who have chosen to repent of the anti-Semitism of the Christian past and who have accepted Israel as an integral part of the contemporary Jewish experience, remain silent on the uprising and Israeli brutality? Or are we all hoping that somehow the situation will dissipate, go unreported, or better still, disappear? This much seems clear: the willingness of Palestinians to endure torture and death and the willingness of Israel to inflict such brutality, point to the most difficult situation, which many choose to ignore: that some basic themes of post-Holocaust Jewish and Christian life are being exposed in a radical and unrelenting way.

If it is true that the occupation of the territories is over, that it has moved beyond occupation to uprising and civil war, then the theological support for the occupation in Jewish Holocaust theology and Christian theologies that lend uncritical support to Israel must end as well. The core of both types of theologies has been shattered. The uprising, therefore, is a crisis on many fronts. It is, at its deepest level, a theological crisis. Of course, like any crisis the uprising presents us with both tragedy and possibility. By demonstrating the truth, even at the price of broken bones and lives, the children of

Palestine force us to think again and to break through ignorance, half-truths, and lies. Will we have the tenacity and courage in safe and comfortable North America that the Palestinian children have on the streets of Gaza and the West Bank? Or, will the inevitable allegations of Jewish self-hate and Christian anti-Jewishness deter us? Are we willing to reexamine our theological presuppositions as particular communities and in dialogue with each other, or will we attempt to pass over the question in silence?

It is not too much to say that the uprising presents the future of Judaism in stark and unremitting terms. The tragedy of the Holocaust is well documented and indelibly ingrained in our consciousness: we know who we were. But do we know who we have become? Contemporary Jewish theology helps us come to grips with our suffering; it hardly recognises that today we are powerful. A theology that holds in tension Holocaust and empowerment speaks eloquently for the victims of Treblinka and Auschwitz yet ignores Sabra and Shatila. It pays tribute to the Warsaw Ghetto uprising but has no place for the uprising of ghetto dwellers on the other side of Israeli power. Jewish theologians insist that the torture and murder of Jewish children be lamented and commemorated in Jewish ritual and belief. It has yet to imagine, though, the possibility that Jews have in turn tortured and murdered

Palestinian children. Holocaust theology relates the story of the Jewish people in its beauty and suffering. Yet it fails to integrate the contemporary history of the Palestinian people as integral to our own. Thus, this theology articulates who we were but no longer helps us understand who we have become.

So some Jews who are trying to reach an understanding of the present have become a contradiction to themselves, while others simply refuse to acknowledge the facts of contemporary Jewish life. A dilemma arises: awareness of Jewish transgression has no theological framework in which to be articulated and acted upon; ignorance (albeit preferred rather than absolute) insists that what is occurring is impossible, that torture and murder are not in fact happening at all, that Jews could not do such things. Jews who become aware have few places to turn theologically, and the ignorant become more and more bellicose in their insistence and in their anger. Meanwhile, despite increasing dissent, Holocaust theology continues as normative in the Jewish community, warning dissident Jews that they approach the terrain of excommunication, and continuing to reinforce the ignorance of many Jews as a theological prerequisite to community membership.[12]

12- For an interesting discussion of the theme of excommunication see Roberta Strauss Feuerlicht, *The Fate of the Jews: A People Town between Israeli Power and Jewish Ethics*, (New York: Times Books, 1983), 281, 282.

As Israel and Jews in diaspora communities become more empowered, this neoconservative trend remains, buttressed by fear, anger, and by a deepening sense of isolation. Anyone who works in the Jewish community recognises this immediately, the almost uncontrollable emotional level that criticism of Israel engenders. To be accused of creating the context for another holocaust is almost commonplace, as are charges of treason and self-hate. It is as if the entire world is still against us, as if the next trains depart for Eastern Europe, as if the death camps remain ready to receive us after an interval of almost half a century. This is why though the entire world outside the United States and Israel understands Yasir Arafat to be a moderate, there is no other name linked by the Jewish community so closely to Adolf Hitler. This is why Prime Minister Shamir spoke of the plans to launch a ship of Palestinian refugees to Israel as an attempt to undermine the state of Israel, as an act of war.[13]

Years after the liberation of the camps, Elie

13- Shamir's response is a prime lesson in Holocaust theology. At a news conference in Jerusalem, Shamir said "It is the height of temerity and hypocrisy that members of the terrorist organization speak of returning. This boat which loads its decks with murderers, terrorists who sought to murder us-all of us, each of us. They wish to bring them to the land of Israel, and demonstrate that they are returning to the same place in which they wished to slay us. We will and do view this as a hostile act, an act which endangers the state of Israel." Quoted in "Israel'.s Furious Over a Palestinian Plan to 'Return' to Haifa by Sail," *New York Times* 11 February, 15.

Wiesel wrote, "Were hatred a solution, the survivors, when they came out of the camps, would have had to burn down the whole world." Surely with the nuclear capacity of Israel, coupled with the sense of isolation and anger, Wiesel's statement remains a caution that may yet be exercised. Is it too much to say that any theology that does not understand the absolute difference between the Warsaw Ghetto and Tel Aviv, between Hitler and Arafat, is a theology that may legitimate that which Wiesel cautioned against?

Christians who have entered into solidarity with the Jewish people are similarly in a dilemma. The road to solidarity has been paved both by Christian renewal, which since Vatican II has been profoundly affected by the recovery of Hebrew Scriptures and the Jewishness of Jesus, and by Holocaust theology, which advises Christians of their anti-Jewishness and their complicity in Jewish suffering and allows a repentance through recognising the centrality of Israel to the Jewish people. Understanding the beauty and suffering of the Jewish people as a call to Christian repentance and transformation hardly prepares the community for a confrontation with Israeli power. How do Christians respond now when, over the years, the centrality of Israel has been stressed as necessary to Christian confession in the arena of dialogue, and no words of criticism against Israel are countenanced as anything but anti-Jewish? Also, Christian Zionism, fundamentalist and liberal, is ever present. What framework do Christians have to probe the history of the state of Israel, to understand the uprising - to question the cost of Jewish empowerment? The challenge for Christian theologies is to articulate a solidarity with the Jewish people that is a critical solidarity, one that recognises the suffering and the power of the Jewish people. By doing this, Christian theologies in the spirit of critical solidarity can open themselves to the suffering of the Palestinian people as a legitimate imperative of what it means to be Christian today.

Clearly the Palestinian struggle for nationhood poses more than the prospect of political negotiation and compromise. For Jews and Christians it presents fundamental theological material that lends depth to the inevitable (though long suffering) political solutions. Without this theological component a political solution may or may not appear. However, the lessons of the conflict would surely be lost and thus the political solution would tend toward superficiality and immediacy rather than depth and longevity. A political solution without a theological transformation would simply enshrine the tragedy to be repeated again. An important opportunity to move beyond our present theologies toward theologies of solidarity, which may usher in a new age of ecumenical cooperation, would be lost. Could it be that the struggle of the Palestinian people - their struggle to be faithful to their history and peoplehood - is a key to the Jewish and Christian struggle to be faithful in the contemporary world?

The torture and death of Palestinian children calls us to a theology that recognises empowerment as a necessary and flawed journey toward liberation. It reminds us that power in and of itself, even for survival, ends in tragedy without the guidance of ethics and a strong sense of solidarity with all those who are struggling for justice. Today, the Palestinian people ask the fundamental question relating to Jewish empowerment: can the Jewish people in Israel, indeed Jews around the world, be liberated without the liberation of the Palestinian people? If we understand the question posed by the Palestinian people, the occupation can no longer continue. What remains is to build a theological framework which delegitimates the torture and the killing - a theology of liberation that sees solidarity as the essence of what it means to be Jewish and Christian.

A new theological framework

The development of a theological framework is crucial to delegitimate torture and murder - that is, to end theologies which promote a myriad of occupations, including, though not limited to, the West Bank and Gaza. In this case we focus on the Israeli occupation as the breakthrough point for Jewish theology. The theological framework which legitimates occupation also, if we look closely, forces Jews to take positions on other issues which would be questioned, even abhorred, if the framework were different. If our theology did not support the occupation, its vision of justice and peace would be transformed. Thus we turn again to the prospect that the uprising represents a culmination and a possibility, if only we seize the moment.

An essential task of Jewish theology should be to reassess the centrality of the state of Israel. To see Israel as an important Jewish community among other Jewish communities, with a historical foundation and evolution, is to legitimate theologically what the Jewish people have acted out with their lives: the continuation of diverse Jewish communities outside the state. Thus the redemptive aspect of Jewish survival after the Holocaust is found in a much broader area than the state of Israel. Reassessing the centrality of Israel hardly means its abandonment. Instead it calls forth a new, more mature relationship. Jews cannot bilocate forever, and the strain of defending policies implemented by others, of criticising without being able to influence directly, of supporting Israel financially, and of being made to feel guilty for not living there, is impossible to continue over a long period of time. With this new understanding, responsibilities between Jewish communities assume a mutuality which includes a critical awareness of the centrality of our ethical tradition as our future. Therefore, the present crisis and any future crisis moves beyond the call for unquestioned allegiance or disassociation from Israel to a critical solidarity with responsibilities and obligations on all sides. To say that we are responsible for one another individually and corporately is, like the centrality of ethics, among our oldest traditions, one that needs to be recovered in a critical way.[14]

14- The strain of this highly problematic relationship has increasingly come to the surface in recent years. Witness the upheavals in North American Jewish life relating to the Lebanese war, the massacres at Sabra and Shatilla, the Pollard spy case and now the uprising. My point is simply that the relationship between Jews in Israel and Jews outside of Israel cannot remain as it is without ultimately dividing the community at its very roots

A parallel task is to deal with the Holocaust in its historical context and to stop brandishing it as a possible future outcome to issues of contemporary Jewish life. The constant use of the Holocaust with reference to Israel is to misjudge and therefore fail to understand the totally different situation of pre- and post-Holocaust Jewry. Pre-Holocaust European Jewry had no state or military; it was truly defenceless before the Nazi onslaught. Israel is a state with superior military ability. Pre-Holocaust European Jewry lived among populations that varied in their attitudes toward Jews from tolerance to hatred. Post-Holocaust Jewry, with its population concentrations in France, England, Canada and the United States, resides in countries where anti-Jewishness is sporadic and inconsequential. Pre-Holocaust Jewry lived among Christians who had as a group little reason to question Christian anti-Jewishness. Post-Holocaust Jewry lives among Christians who have made repeated public statements, writings, even ritual affirmations of the centrality of the Jewish people and Christian culpability for an anti-Jewish past. The differences between pre- and post-Holocaust Jewry can be listed on many other levels as well, which is not to deny that anti-Jewishness continues to exist. As many Jewish writers have pointed out, the paradox is that the most dangerous place for Jews to live today is in the state of Israel rather than the Jewish centres of Europe and North America.

Even in relation to Israel the application of Holocaust language is clearly inappropriate. Israel has been involved in two wars since 1967 and can claim an undisputed victory in neither; no civilian life was lost outside the battlefield. The great fear, repeated over and over again, is that one day Israel will lose a war and that the civilian population will be annihilated - i.e., will experience another holocaust. It is important to note here that, if the situation continues as it is today, it is inevitable that one day Israel will lose a war and face the possibility of annihilation. No nation is invincible forever, no empire exists that is not destined to disappear, there is no country that does not, at some point in its history, lose badly and suffer immensely. Can our present theology exempt Israel from the reality of shifting alliances, military strategies, and political life? The only way to prevent military defeat is to make peace when you are powerful. Of course, even here there is never any absolute protection from persecution. But if military defeat does come and if the civilian population is attacked, the result, though tragic, will not be, by any meaningful definition, another holocaust. And it would not, by any means, signal the end of the Jewish people, as many Holocaust theologians continue to speculate. It would be a terrible event, too horrible to mention, except that we must discuss it in order to prevent it. The differences between the Holocaust and any future military defeat of Israel would be too obvious to explore, and would hardly need exploration if our present theology was not confused on this most important point.

To reassess the centrality of the state of Israel and distinguish the historical event of Holocaust from the situation of contemporary Jewish life is imperative to the third task of Jewish theology, the redefinition of Jewish identity. This is an incredibly difficult and complex task whose parameters can only be touched upon here. Yet it is the most crucial of areas, raising the essential question that each generation faces: what does it mean to be Jewish in the contemporary world?

There is little question that Holocaust theology is the normative theology of the Jewish community today and that at the centre of this theology is the Holocaust and the state of Israel. Rabbinic theology, the normative Jewish theology for almost two millennia, initially sought to continue as if neither the Holocaust nor the state of Israel were central to the Jewish people. Reform Judaism, the interesting, sometimes shallow, nineteenth century attempt to come to grips with modern life, also sought to bypass the formative events of our time. Yet after the Holocaust, and especially since the Six Day War in 1967, both theological structures have been transformed with an underlying Holocaust theology. Secular Jews, as well, often affiliated with progressive politics and economics, have likewise experienced a shifting framework of interpretation. Though not explicitly religious, their aid has been solicited by Holocaust theologians to build the state of Israel as the essential aspect of belonging to the Jewish people. In sum, both those who believed in Jewish particularly and those who sought a more universal identification have increasingly derived their Jewish identity from the framework of Holocaust and Israel. And there is little reason to believe that any of these frameworks - Orthodox, Reform, or secular humanistic - can ever again return to its pre-Holocaust, pre-Israel position.

We can only move ahead by affirming the place of the Holocaust and Israel as important parts of Jewish identity while insisting that they are not and cannot become the sum total of what it means to be Jewish. The point here is to take the dynamic of Holocaust and Israel and understand it in new ways. In both events there is, among other things, an underlying theme of solidarity, which has been buried in our anger and isolation. This includes solidarity with our own people - resistance in the Warsaw Ghetto, for example, as well as the mutual support found in the empowerment of the Jewish people after the Holocaust - as well as others who have come into solidarity with us, including the small, courageous minority of Christians during the Holocaust who helped Jews at the risk of their lives, and those Christians who supported Jews in the difficult post-war years. As importantly, if we recover our own history, there is a theme of Jewish solidarity with others, including Palestinians, even in times of great danger. The latter includes some of the early settlers and intellectuals involved in the renewal of the Jewish community in Palestine, well-known figures like Judah Magnes, Hannah Arendt, Martin Buber, and many others.[15]

Even during the Holocaust there were voices, the Dutch Jew Etty Hillesum, for one, who argued that Jewish suffering should give birth to a world of mutuality and solidarity so that no people should ever suffer again. As she voluntarily accompanied her people to Auschwitz, Hillesum was hardly a person who went like a lamb to her slaughter. Rather, she chose a destiny as an act of solidarity with her own people and the world. Is it possible that those who affirmed human dignity where it was most difficult and those who argued, and continue to argue today, for reconciliation with the Palestinian people even with the risks involved, represent the only future worth bequeathing to our children? By emphasising our dignity and solidarity we appropriate the event of the Holocaust and Israel as

---

15- For Hannah Arendt'.s prophetic understanding of the choices facing the Jewish settlers in Palestine see a collection of her essays *Hannah Arendt, the Jew as Pariab Jewish Identity and Politics in the Modern Age,* ed. Ron H Feldman (New York: Grove Press, 1978).

formative in a positive and critical way. Thus they ask us once again to embrace the world with the hope that our survival is transformative for our own people and the world.

The key to a new Jewish identity remains problematic unless we understand that deabsolutising Israel, differentiating Holocaust from the contemporary Jewish situation, and recovering the history of solidarity within our tradition and with those outside it, lead us to a critical confrontation with our empowerment. To celebrate our survival is important; to realise that our empowerment has come at a great cost is another thing altogether. Can we at the fortieth anniversary of the state of Israel realise that the present political and religious sensibilities can only lead to disaster? Can we argue openly that the issue of empowerment is much broader than that of an exclusive Jewish state and that other options, including mutual autonomy with confederation, may be important to contemplate for the fiftieth anniversary of Israel? Can we openly declare that as American Jews we can no longer ask our government to support a foreign policy that contradicts the ethical heart of what it means to be Jewish? Can we, in good conscience and faith, appeal to Christians, Palestinians, and people of good will around the world to help us end the occupation and, if we do not heed the call, to force us to stop for our own sake?

For this is the place we have arrived, well beyond the pledge of loyalty and the private criticism that have abounded for so many years. The uprising challenges the power of the Israeli government and the heart of the Jewish people. But the power to inflict injury and death remains. And therefore the power to change our history, to redefine our inheritance, to alter what it means to be Jewish, continues in the hands of those who would see the occupation continue. And with the occupation are a myriad of policies around the world that bring only shame to those who invoke the victims of the Holocaust to legitimate terror.

With the uprising we have lost our innocence; Jewish theology must begin with this loss. A weak and helpless people has arisen with a power that surprises and now saddens us. A people set apart returns to the history of nations less a beacon than as a fellow warrior, living at the expense of others, almost forfeiting its sense of purpose. The commanding voices of Sinai and of Auschwitz beckon us to struggle to reclaim the ethical witness of the Jewish people.

CHAPTER TWO

Beyond the Jewish - Christian dialogue: solidarity with the Palestinian people

Some time ago I received a phone call from a young Jewish progressive thinker inviting me to give a short reflection at a gathering commemorating the eighth anniversary of the massacres at the Palestinian refugee camps of Sabra and Shatilla in West Beirut, Lebanon. These massacres took place in September 1982, after the Israeli invasion of Lebanon, and claimed at least 800 lives; the actual death toll may have been considerably higher.

As I recall, the invitation came in the middle of the conversation and, with my acceptance, we simply continued on. I accepted the invitation as I accept most invitations: taking note of the date and time, inquiring about the expected length of the talk and the likely composition of the audience.

After our phone conversation, I took a walk and within minutes I was shaken by the prospect of addressing the enormity of Sabra and Shatilla. If

Palestinians were present, I wondered how they would feel about a Jew addressing their dead, about this atrocity which in reality and symbolically helps define their experience of the Jewish people.

Would I, like many Jewish spokespersons, mention the suffering, then point out, as had been affirmed by the Kahan Commission appointed to investigate the massacres, Israel's "indirect responsibility," lament the rise of Menachem Begin and Ariel Sharon as aberrations within the Zionist enterprise, and then proceed to analyse the damage of such events to the Jewish soul? And what would Jews in the audience want or expect of me: to be critical of Israel then and now, but to hold to that tenuous line- as the contemporary Jewish thinker David Biale describes the litmus test of authentic Jewish progressives - between the two rights of Jews and Palestinians to the land, always being careful when pointing out current Israeli "rejectionism" that the "original sin," in his eyes, was Palestinian rejectionism?[1]

And from a religious viewpoint, would Jews want or expect me to demonstrate the "anguish" of the Israeli Jewish theologian David Hartman, or assent to the recent essay of the American Jewish theologian Arthur Waskow, who refers to the land as

---

[1] - For a somewhat typical response of Jewish progressives to criticism of Israel see David Biale, "The Philo-Semitic Face of Christian Anti-Semitism," *Tikkun 4* (May/June, 1989): 99-102:

being twice blessed, to Jews and Palestinians, while at the same time arguing even at this late date, in the midst of the brutal suppression of the Palestinian uprising, that we, the Jewish people, are a vanguard people?

And how could I articulate to the audience of Jews and Palestinians that the problem, in my mind, was less Begin, Sharon and Shamir, though they were indeed problematic, but Jewish progressives like Hartman and Waskow, as well as others like Michael Walzer, a Jewish ethicist at the institute for Advanced Studies at Princeton, and Abba Eban, the Israeli diplomat. For these progressives are the ones who, before and after Sabra and Shatilla, who before and during the Palestinian uprising, define the parameters of dissent - the realm of thinkable thought - the borderline for which excommunication is invoked, and thus, in Noam Chomsky's analysis, become experts in legitimation.[2]

Of course, in another sense the unthinkable has already been both thought and done from the beginning, and the massacres at Sabra and Shatilla-surrounded, as these camps were, by the Israeli aerial bombardments and napalming common in Lebanon - were less an aberration than a

---

2- For the profile of David Hartman see Michael Kramer, "Sage in a Land of Anger," *Time*, April 30, 1990, p. 90-91. Also see Arthur Waskow, "Twice Promised Land," *Tikkun* 5 (September/October, 1990): 56-58.

continuity with the mass atrocities and expulsions of Palestinians in 1948, the Qibya massacre of 1953, the expulsions, occupation and annexation of 1967, and, of course, the terror, deportations and atrocities since December 1987. And all this has been combined with a methodical, systematic, bureaucratic and, from the Israeli side, completely legal process of expropriation and displacement. At this level the massacres of Sabra and Shatilla, like Deir Yassin in 1948, the Ami Popper incident in May 1990 and the October 1990 massacres at the Dome of the Rock, planned and unplanned, whether by the Jewish underground, the Israeli regular forces, or individual actions, all take on an almost sinister logic: to make it clear that no Palestinians living in historic Palestine are safe, and that any dream of return to Palestine will issue into the nightmare of massive dislocation and death.[3]

3- Documentation of the combination of physical terror and bureaucratic expropriation is found in **Punishing a Nation: Human Rights Violations During the Palestinian Uprising, December 1987-1988** (Palestine: Al Haq, 1988).

Jewish progressives and the Palestinians

Many years ago in his book *The Rebel*, Albert Camus wrote that when "crime dons the apparel of innocence, it is innocence which is called upon to justify itself," and we must say that over the years it is Jewish progressives in America who have been called upon to justify, to defend, to, if necessary, lie about this continuing criminality. And in many ways it is Jewish progressives in America who have justified and defended the Jewish progressives in Israel who have been the architects of these policies from the beginning - David Ben Gurion, Golda Meir, Shimon Peres, Yitzak Rabin as examples - that is the Labour party rather than Likud. The best of all possible worlds, of course, is the progressive Jewish Israeli who can speak as a bridge for the American Jewish progressive community: people like Abba Eban and the Israeli "peace camp."

The overall message which emanates from the

progressive spokespersons, at least of late, is clear: all is not well; keep the faith. Surely this is the message of Abba Eban in his introduction to the English language publication of the Kahan Commission report on the Sabra and Shatilla massacres. For Eban, an aberration occurred which Jewish conscience could not bury. Admitting "indirect" responsibility, the Commission itself and the demonstrations which forced the inquiry all in Eban's eyes are a testimony to the strength and vibrancy of Israeli democracy. To be sure, according to Eban, other peoples, especially the Palestinians, lack such conscience and fortitude. However, the overall Zionist enterprise is necessary and proper: the strength of Israeli democracy allows for mid-course corrections.[4]

As eloquent and persuasive as Eban's analysis is for some Jews, the more powerful complement is furnished by the legitimation offered by those theologians who provide the framework of Holocaust theology to justify the almost unqualified and unequivocal support of Israel. One such Orthodox Holocaust theologian is Rabbi Irving Greenberg, director of the New York City Jewish Center for Learning and Leadership, who sees the Jewish prophetic critique as growing out of Jewish powerlessness and a continuation of that critique

---

4- Abba Eban, intr. **The Beirut Massacre: The Complete Kahan Commission Report** (New York: Karz-Cohl, 1983), V.-XVI.

with the assumption of power as both naive and dangerous. The warning is clear: the prophetic within empowerment might accomplish again what the enemies of the Jews have already accomplished once - holocaust. For Greenberg, the necessity of a new Jewish ethic involves the articulation and acceptance of the "normalisation" of the Jewish condition and the correction of aberrations, among them the massacres at Sabra and Shatilla. On the Lebanese war, initiated by Israel, which claimed 10-20,000 Palestinian and Lebanese lives, Greenberg concludes in a characteristic way: "The war was wrong but well within the parameters of error and breakdown which characterise normal, healthy, moral democracies."[5]

This analysis by Greenberg was written in March 1988 in an essay titled, "The Ethics of Jewish Power." Thus his reflection on Lebanon takes place within the context of the Palestinian uprising, to which he applies a similar standard: correct the abuse; keep the faith. And like Eban in his analysis of Sabra and Shatilla, Greenberg mentions the massacres, the dead and the dying Palestinians of Lebanon, the West Bank and Gaza, within the

---

5- Irving Greenberg, "The Ethics of Jewish Power, **Perspectives** (New York: National Jewish Center of Learning and Leadership, 1988) 10. For entended analysis of Holocaust theology see Marc H. Ellis, **Toward a Jewish Theology of Liberation: The Uprising and the Future** (Maryknoll, New York: Orbis, 1989) and Marc H. Ellis, **Beyond Innocece and Redemption: Confronting the Holocaust and Israel Power** (San Francisco: Harper and Row, 1990.)

context of Jewish moral conscience, Jewish democracy and Jewish strength. The drama is Jewish; the Palestinians are peripheral, and since the drama is essentially religious, having to do with the innocence and redemption of the Jewish people, the Palestinians are the "others" who block this eschatological vision. As for centuries the central "other" who blocked the Christian drama in the West, we Jews should be aware of the possible consequences which may be and perhaps already are far beyond the "corrective" scenario of Eban and Greenberg.[6]

But what if one finds that the understanding of the "normalisation" of the Jewish people is abnormal and unacceptable? What if one comes to believe that the aberration is in fact longstanding and continuing and that any correction will be within the framework of continuity rather than a radical change of direction? What if the essence of the Israeli state is expansion rather than democracy, and the Jewish character of the state makes expendable, in a terrifying sense, makes logical the ghettoisation of indigenous Palestinian culture and community in historic Palestine? What if one believes that what we are witnessing today is the culmination of a sixty-year process in which Palestinian culture and peoplehood are undermined in historic Palestine.

6- Ibid.

And what if one believes that the end of Palestine signals the end of the Jewish tradition as we have known and inherited it?

If all this is true, then we can draw the following conclusions: that the survival of Palestinian people, while dependent on many factors, is also partially dependent on progressive Jews moving beyond the acceptable levels of Jewish dissent; that the progressive Jewish dissenting community must realise that in fact Eban, Walzer, Hartman, Biale, Waskow, Greenberg, et. al. - in short the old boys network of Jewish progressives, resurrected and infused with energy by Michael Lerner's new journal *Tikkun* - is not with regard to the Palestinian people progressive at all. Operating from a political and ethical high ground, involved almost exclusively in a now more defensive but still rigorous vanguard mentality, the Jewish progressive consensus position is a form of oppression vis-a-vis the Palestinian people. Finally, it is important to understand that the Jewish progressive tradition as we know it can live with the expansion and expulsions of 1948 and 1967, as Martin Buber and Abba Eban did, and with the massacres of Sabra and Shatilea, as Elie Wiesel did, with the policy of might and beatings, as David Hartman and Irving Greenberg did. Simply put: corrections, anguish over Israeli policies, or arguments for the Jewish soul, are not enough.[7]

7- For a discussion of the Jewish tradition of dissent and its limitation see Ellis, *Beyond Innocence*,

I am quite well aware that at this point a truly progressive position may fail in its test with Jewish state power in Israel, and of course this has been part of the anguish quotient in Jewish politics and theology - feeling forced to defend policies that many can hardly support and no one outside the state apparatus can control. Thus breaking completely with these policies and with the role of legitimation cannot guarantee success. That is, we are dealing with state power, Jewish in this case, which is bent on diminishing the Palestinian presence in historic Palestine.

At this juncture there seem only two possibilities to control Jewish state power in Israel: call for and actively pursue the end of U.S. aid to Israel; force the end of Israeli occupation through military intervention. Though these two positions often occasion an hysterical reaction, in reality they simply represent the flip side of Greenberg's understanding of normalisation: an occupying power, once given the possibility of voluntary withdrawal, must then face political, diplomatic, economic and military sanctions. In this light the link made between Iraqi occupation of Kuwait and the Israeli occupation of the West Bank and Gaza becomes less farfetched than often portrayed in the Western media. Thus a truly progressive Jewish position must take into account these realities, which is to say that we are unable to, indeed we refuse to live with the inevitability of the end that the Israeli state proposes.

With these propositions suggested, I would advance five statements, endless in their complexity, which may give form to a more honest progressive Jewish position:

- *What Jews have done to the Palestinians since the establishment of the state of Israel in 1948 is wrong.

- *In the process of conquering and displacing the Palestinian people, Jews have done what has been done to us over two millennia.

- *In this process Jews have become almost everything we loathe about our oppressors.

- *It is only in confronting state power in Israel that Jews can move beyond being victim or oppressor.

- *The movement beyond victimisation and oppression can only come through a solidarity with those whom we as Jews have displaced: the Palestinian people.

Clearly the inability of Jewish progressives to make these statements continues today even after the close of the Gulf War. The example of Yossi Sarid and other Peace Now activists in their abandonment of the Palestinians for "supporting Iraq" shows the shallowness of their position with regard to justice for the Palestinian people.

Solidarity with the Palestinian people

What does this solidarity with the Palestinian people mean today? What are the foundational visions which may shape this concept of solidarity into flesh and blood reality?

The first step, of course, is to abandon the two-rights understanding, as if the question of Jews and Palestinians is a symmetrical one. Whatever one wants to argue from the Jewish side vis-a-vis Jewish history - our difficult history in Europe which gave rise to Zionism and the culmination of that history in the Holocaust, which provided the final impetus for the birth of the Jewish state - the effect for the Palestinians has been brutal, even catastrophic.

A.B. Yehoshua, the Jewish Israeli novelist, writes that the "concept of historic right has no objective moral validity when applied to the return of the Jewish people to its land." Rather, as a committed Zionist, Yehoshua argues that the Jewish people has a "full moral right to seize part of Eretz Israel, or any other land, even by force," on the basis of a right he calls the survival right of the endangered. His underlying proposition is as follows: "A nation without a homeland has the right to take, even by force, part of the homeland of another nation, and to establish its sovereignty there." Thus Yehoshua, unlike most Jewish progressives, admits of what might be termed a necessary theft, a "moral invasion"as it were. But to hold the Palestinians responsible for resisting that theft or to expect them to accept it is in Yehoshua's eyes ridiculous, as is the extension of that theft to the rest of historic Palestine in the possible annexation of the occupied territories.

For Yehoshua, the basis for the Jewish right is the seizure of a part, and thus if Jews intend to extricate themselves from the "situation of a people without a homeland by turning another people into a nation without a homeland, our right to survival will turn to dust in our hands."[8]

Whatever one thinks of Yehoshua's foundational argument that the survival of the Jewish people is linked to a territorial sovereignty - a position that should be probed in a deep way by Jewish thinkers - his two-rights position moves well beyond the typical expression of Jewish innocence and Palestinian demonism. Though his book bears the English title *Between Right and Right*, his argument

---

8- A.B Yehoshua, **Betvween Right and Right: Israel, Problem or Solution?** trans. Arnold Schwartz (Garden City, New York: Doubleday, 1981) 101, 105.

speaks of Jewish necessity, the dispersal of Palestinians, and the right of Palestinians to resist. Thus, the title might be better rendered as *Between Jewish Necessity and Palestinian Rights to a Homeland.* Accordingly, it could be that the formation of Israel was necessary in its historical moment and at the same time wrong vis-a-vis the Palestinian people. The original sin, then, was European anti-semitism, not Palestinian resistance to a Jewish state. But even here, if one accepts Yehoshua's analysis of historical necessity in seizing only a part of the land, the framework he maintains is strictly separatist. That is, the necessity of survival, the formation of a Jewish state, is extended beyond the historical moment into a relentless future: to survive physically and culturally Jews must be separate in their own land for the remainder of world history. The moral invasion is to flee the fire and to build a new home among others who have fled the same fire. Those who fled the Jewish fire must rebuild their own homes somewhere else.[9]

Here the "two state" position, while seemingly progressive and argued from a survivalist or innocent perspective, needs to be questioned within the framework of solidarity. The entire burden of proof is placed on the Palestinians. For example, the two-state position as argued by most Jews, including

---

9- A.B Yehoshua, **Betvween Right and Right: Israel, Problem or Solution?** trans. Arnold Schwartz (Garden City, New York: Doubleday, 1981) 107-147.

Yehoshua and others like Yossi Sarid, places primary responsibility on the Palestinians to, among other things, demonstrate their ability to live peacefully with Israel, to renounce their fundamental claims of sovereignty over all of Palestine, to guarantee a demilitarised state with Israeli security positions within Palestine and the right of Israeli invasion if militarisation occurs. At the same time, it also limits forever the size of Palestine to one fifth its original land mass in the least fertile part of Palestine. Among other things, it assumes, at a foundational level, that Israelis should be afraid of Palestinians but Palestinians have nothing to fear from Israelis, a position that many Palestinians in their diaspora no doubt find surprising, if not untenable. [10]

Though a two-state solution may be the only practical possibility at the moment, it falls far short of the solidarity requisite to the crisis which confronts both sides. Most Jewish progressives, for instance, see the two-state solution as a way of ridding themselves of the Palestinian "problem" demographically and morally. Give them their state and Jews are free of a possible Palestinian majority, hence the preservation of the Jewish state; Jews are also morally cleansed of having expelled, beaten,

---

10- These themes are annunciated most clearly as a consensus progressive Jewish position by Michael Lerner, editor of the journal **Tikkun.** See Lerner, "The Occupation: Immoral and Stupid," **Tikkun** 3 (March/ April 1988): 7-12.

tortured and murdered Palestinians, thereby protecting the purity of the Jewish soul. The position is clear as Amos Oz, the Jewish Israeli novelist, describes it: granting a divorce between Jews and Palestinians. The image is equally clear: separate Jewish and Palestinian states with a wall so high that Jews will never have to see another Palestinian. Palestinians will be banished from Jewish history.[11]

The desire to preserve, or rather reassert Jewish innocence by banishing the victims of Jewish oppression is understandable and inadequate. It allows Jews to retreat from the confrontation with Palestinians and within themselves as if the bloodshed had not occurred. By allowing Jews to see themselves in their pre-state identity, they ignore the brutality Jews are capable of, thus ignoring Jewish post-state reality. That Jewish history in Palestine is covered with blood through our contemporary oppression of Palestinians is a lesson absolutely necessary for Jews as a people. We cannot come to grips with our recent history unless we see the Palestinians now as intimate to our self-identity and capabilities as a people. That is, the victims of Jewish power are as intimate to us as we are to those who oppressed us. Confronting the Jewish abuse of power is impossible without the

---

11- Amos Oz, "Make Peace, Not Love," **American-Israeli Civil Liberties Coalition** 10 (Summer 1990): 15.

physical preservation of Palestine in our midst, and the prospect of Jewish healing both in its trauma of European mass murder and in its trauma of beating and expelling another people cannot be worked out alone.

Progressive proponents of the two-state solution seek to banish the bad Jewish conscience in a way that delays a reckoning with the history Jews have created. Thus a genuine Jewish progressive position is dependent on moving beyond the state of Israel and the state of Palestine into a genuine vision of confederation which allows both autonomy and integration of Jews and Palestinians.

Of course this also leaves open the possibility of a Palestinian return to parts of Palestine that would be closed off in a two-state scenario. If genuine solidarity is to be gleaned, then the Palestinians have a right to be healed of their own trauma of displacement, thus allowing a new perspective on their own catastrophe. Only a Palestinian right to return can authenticate what the Palestinian educator, Muhammed Hallaj, has written of as the interlocking destiny of Jew and Palestinian. In short the argument for the possibility of Jewish and Palestinian life together in historic Palestine moves beyond the typical Jewish progressive concern for Jewish purity and innocence by envisioning a future which recovers the deepest ethical impulses of the Jewish people in confrontation with the reality of Jewish history.[12]

But arguing from the Jewish perspective does not in the least diminish the Palestinian recovery by placing it solely within the Jewish framework. The Palestinian future is for Palestinians authentic and self-generating. Their desire or refusal to live with Jews is, of course, their decision to make within the context of Palestinian history. Jewish life as interlocking with Palestinian life is an absolute necessity from the Jewish perspective but is, in my view, entirely optional from the Palestinian perspective of living on the other side of Jewish power.

Solidarity with the Palestinian people moves beyond romanticisation and demonisation. Solidarity with the Jewish people in Europe was an ethical and practical necessity not because all Jews were beautiful, but because Jews as a people were innocent. As documented by many Jewish historians, the Jewish ghettos had heroes, ordinary citizens, criminals and collaborators. The behaviour of Jews toward other Jews ran the gamut of great charity to unbridled brutality and, of course, everything in

---

12- For the development of this theme see Muhammed Hallaj, "The Palestinian Dream: The Democratic Secuar State," in Rosemary Radford Ruether and Marc H. Ellis, **Beyond Occupation: American Jewish, Christian and Palestinian Voices For Peace** (Boston: Beacon, 1990) 220-230.

between. And the Palestinians are no doubt similar in regard to their complexity and, in this situation, their innocence.

Hence Jewish progressives often want it both ways: a retroactive demand of rescue of a Jews during the Holocaust, coupled with no discussion of Jewish internal realities outside of the framework of innocence. Similarly, they reject any connection between Jewish rescue and Jewish behaviour just a decade after the Holocaust, or even today, but find it surprisingly easy to take to task Palestinians with regard to the policies of the Palestinian Liberation Organisation, the Palestinian reaction to Iraq's invasion of Kuwait, and in general anything that seems to compromise Palestinian innocence from a Jewish perspective. They also constantly link the Palestinian struggle for liberation with the policies of a future Palestinian state, as if the unknown future should determine the level of support for the current struggle. Thus as Jews we rightly shift the burden of proof to those who oppressed us, but in a strange twist we now continually shift the burden of proof to those whom we are oppressing.[13]

13- On the diversity and complexity of Jewish behavior in the ghettos of Eastern Europe see Isaiah Trunk, **Judenrat: The Jewish Councils in Eastern Europe Under Nazi Occupation** (New York: Stein and Day, 1977). For a dialogue on the shifting of the burden onto Palestinians see "Special Focus on Iraq," **Tikkum** 5 (November/December 1990): 48-78

To accept this analysis is to radically change the Jewish perception of the Israeli-Palestinian conflict, from two rights to wrong and right; from aberration to continuity; from the need for "corrections" to a radical critical evaluation. As important, and as difficult, at least for Jewish progressives, is the radical reevaluation of Jewish self-understanding these statements imply. Israel is not innocent, and neither are we; our claims on suffering are now forfeited. Our claim to choseness, even in a secularised form, has become irritating rather than compelling. Israel is not redemptive, and neither is Jewish empowerment. Instead Israel, and for that matter the politicised use of the Holocaust, is a burden to the Jewish people and the Palestinian people as well. The question of Israel and the remembrance of the Holocaust so central to Jewish identity have become something other than expected, have we. Is it possible to see ourselves as a people organised to destroy another people without radically reevaluating who we have become as a people? And if we have betrayed our suffering and our empowerment is built on the blood of others, where are we to turn to in order to reconstruct a way of being Jewish in which we can recognise our own faces and hearts and realise the deepest impulses of the Jewish people?

This is the task before us, one that will need the skills of politics, ethics and theology to successfully realise. In his 1968 analysis of the imperatives of the Holocaust, Emil Fackenheim, one of the more noted Jewish Holocaust theologians, emphasised the need for sheer survival of the Jewish people in order to face the questions of Jewish history and a possible Jewish future. Today, just two decades later, in a way that Fackenheim could not then and does not today understand, in a momentous inversion, the survival of the Palestinian people provides the possibility of a Jewish future. This is no doubt what the German Catholic theologian Johann Baptist Metz had in mind when he envisioned the future of Christians and Jews after the Holocaust in these words: "We Christians can never go back behind Auschwitz: to go beyond Auschwitz, if we see clearly, is impossible for us by ourselves. It is possible only together with the victims of Auschwitz." In light of Sabra and Shatila and the Palestinian uprising, these words assume a new meaning relating to the common journey of Jew and Palestinian. For Jews the challenge might be stated thus: "We Jews can never go back behind empowerment; to go beyond empowerment, if we see clearly, is impossible for us by ourselves. It is possible only with the victims of our empowerment, the Palestinian people."[14]

14- Johann Baptist Metz, *The Emergent* **Church: The Future of Christianity in a Posbourgeois Word,** trans. Peter Mann (New York: Crossroad, 1981) 19.

Christian theology and the Palestinian uprising

Though some Jews are willing to move beyond the Jewish progressive consensus, they remain unorganised, a small minority without public voice. And those who might provide solidarity and a platform for Jewish dissent, that is progressive Christians, are too often aligned with the progressive Jewish consensus. This union of progressive Jews and Christians was formed after the Holocaust and especially after the Second Vatican Council, which gave birth to the contemporary ecumenical dialogue.

As pursued over the last decades, the ecumenical dialogue has concerned itself with a variety of issues, including, among others, covenant, salvation, and civil rights. But the main aspects of the dialogue remain today what they were in the beginning: anti-semitism and Israel. The foundation of the dialogue rests on Christian repentance for anti-Jewishness and acceptance of Israel as central to Jewish identity. Those involved in the dialogue know that it has essentially turned into what one might call the ecumenical deal: eternal repentance for Christian anti-Jewishness unencumbered by any substantive criticism of Israel. Substantive criticism of Israel means, at least from the Jewish side, the reemergence of Christian anti-Jewishness.[15]

In this ecumenical deal Zionism and Judaism are essentially linked, and the main energy of ecumenical gatherings is spent on diverting the question that hovers over all discussions of Jews and Christians: the oppression of the Palestinian people by Jewish Israelis with the support, by commission or omission, of Jewish and Christian partners in the ecumenical dialogue. The ecumenical dialogue, or if you will, the ecumenical deal, continues as a way to manage Christian dissent on the issue of Israel and Palestine by brandishing the potent club of anti-Jewishness.

The paradox is that just as Jewish progressives and career ecumenical dialoguers like former director of the Synagogue Council of America, Rabbi Marc Tannebaum, provide the cover for Israeli policy, Christian progressives, who joined the dialogue out of repentance, also enter into complicity against indigenous Palestinian culture and presence in historic Palestine. Jewish progressives provide

---

15- For a discussion of the ecumenical deal in church circles see Marc H. Ellis, Ecumenical Deal and the Bishops Middle East Statement, *"Ecumenical Trends"* 19 (March 1990): 33-36.

the good face of Jews and Israel which Christians accept and, in a strange twist, desperately need. Adjustments are made, of course, when specific incidents are too horrible to be accepted, and then Jewish and Christian progressives share a particular and short-lived anguish, which paradoxically strengthens the bond of these dialoguers as they attempt to navigate the issue of Jews and Israel through a difficult period. Any Christian who moves beyond anguish into a critical confrontation with Israeli policy, demanding, for example, the end of the occupation, is jettisoned from the rarefied atmosphere of the dialogue or simply find no Jews to speak with. Any Jew who has engaged in substantive pubic criticism of Israel is not allowed in the dialogue at all. Thus well meaning Christians are, like Jewish progressives, in complicity with the diminution and ghettoisation of Palestinian life.[16]

Those Christians who realise, even dimly, that the relationship of Jews and Christians has changed dramatically rarely know how to speak of the present reality. They are literally without a framework, theological or otherwise, to analyse, let alone articulate the end of Jewish innocence. What does the ecumenical dialogue look like if Christians no longer oppress Jews and if Jews actually oppress

---

16- The reality of ethnocide has prompted me to call for an end to the ecumenical dialogue. See Marc H. Ellis, "End This Dialogue," **Tablet 224** (June 30, 1990): 810. Also see East, "**Cristianity and Crisis 50** (July 2, 1990): 211-212.

Palestinians? Where does the ecumenical discussion move if Jews are not powerless but rather are powerful and too often use that power to subjugate another people?

Christian theologians have offered little guidance in this area. For example, Roy Eckardt of Lehigh University, and Paul van Buren of Temple University have written poignantly about Jewish suffering in European history and beautifully about the Christian need to recover Jewish roots and face the Jewish people as a living reality. Yet in so doing they have, despite protests to the contrary, romanticised Jews and the Jewish tradition and placed critique of Israel at a superficial level of policy analysis, which mitigates against a radical probing of the central dynamic of Jewish Israeli existence: the diminution of Palestinian presence in historic Palestine. In short, Eckardt and van Buren replicate the Jewish progressive consensus of Eban, Walzer and Hartman: the drama of Holocaust and Israel is Jewish, having to do with Jewish suffering and empowerment. For Eckardt and van Buren, the Palestinians are peripheral, almost absent. For better or worse, Palestinians must accept this Jewish drama because of historic Christian anti-Jewishness. In general, Christian theologians provide little if any help in articulating what everybody, especially Palestinians, know: that Jews without power can be demonised and romanticised by Christians but it remains almost impossible for Christians to accept that Jews, having taken power, are doing exactly to Palestinians what was done to them by Christians.[17]

Robert McAfee Brown, Professor Emeritus at Pacific School of Religion in California, is another Christian theologian whose work has been affected both by the Holocaust and more recently by the Israeli-Palestinian conflict. His earlier involvement with the Holocaust is most evident in his study *Elie Wiesel: Messenger to All Humanity*, in which Brown attempts to immerse himself in the Holocaust world of death and destruction. Clearly Brown, a Presbyterian, sees the Holocaust as a challenge to Jews and Christians, indeed the entire world. For Brown, the Holocaust confronts the world and especially Christians with moral dilemmas posed in the form of questions. "How could a decent people with the highest form of Western culture engage in the murder of six million Jews? How could the world remain silent as the Jews were slaughtered? How can the world remain indifferent today, when similar horrors loom on the horizon? How can we believe in human goodness or God after the Holocaust and in the face of the difficult challenges confronting us today?" For Brown, listening to

---

17- For an early discussion of these themes, see A. Roy Eckardt, **Elder and Younger Brothers: The Encounter of Jews and Christians** (New York: Charles Scribner's Sons, 1967). Also see Paul M. Van Buren, **A Christian Theology of the People Israel**, Part II (New York: Seabury, 1983,.

voices from the Holocaust provides insight into these questions; but more, it forces a confrontation with some of the most difficult questions of twentieth-century life. Though it is impossible for Brown and others who were not in the death camps to enter into the world of the Holocaust, it is possible to allow the Holocaust to enter their world. This is a shattering experience, but Brown believes it is only through taking the risk of listening to the stories of the Holocaust that the ability to celebrate life may be reclaimed.[18]

With Brown's respect for Jewish suffering in mind, and his continuous gestures of solidarity with the Jewish people and with Israel over the years, it is interesting to see his latest commentary on the uprising, titled "Christians in the West Must Confront the Middle East." As a person known for his prophetic writings about many areas of the word, Brown's reluctance to criticise Israel has been obvious both to those who await his words and to himself. In the first place, Brown has been reluctant to speak because of Jewish suffering and Christian complicity in that suffering, the understanding of which has "cast a heavy shadow over my view of the

---

18- Robert McAfee Brown, *Elie Wiesel: Messenger to All Humanity* (Notre Dame: Univ. of Notre Dame Press, 1983), 2-3. Brown dedicated his book to Wiesel; it reads in part: "You have said that to be a Jew means to testify; such must also be the obligation of a Christian. And you have taught us all-Jews, Christians and all Humanity- that before testifying ourselves, we must listen to your testimony. And ..to testify."

world, my understanding of God, any estimate of human nature and my theology of the church." In a world devoid of affirmations of Jews and Judaism, Israel has been a source of affirmation for Jews and therefore worthy of support. For Brown, the limitation of this approach is that it fails to take with equal seriousness the rights of Palestinians, their displacement from the land, and the oppressive conditions under which they have been forced to live ever since.

The second reason for Brown's reluctance to speak is that the Holocaust was only the latest of almost two thousand years of Christian anti-Jewishness; a challenge to the existence of the state of Israel almost certainly will be interpreted as a continuation of that history, thus earning him the label anti-Semitic. For Brown, the shortcomings of this approach lie in the failure of all involved to distinguish clearly enough between the religious faith, Judaism, and the modern political entity, Israel.

A final reason for silence is a Christian desire not to aid in any way "enemies of Israel who are anti-Semitic, terrorist, chauvinistic, unreasoning, or all of the above." Brown sees that the shortcoming here is the failure to distinguish between fanatical criticism and creative criticism; a terrain for public discourse must have options beyond supporting either Palestinian displacement or Israeli annihilation. In sum, Brown finds himself caught between two concerns, both legitimate and difficult to resolve: the commitment to Israel because of past Christian anti-Jewishness, and the commitment to the liberation of all oppressed people arising from Christian faith, a commitment that must include Jews in the past and Palestinians in the present.[19]

What allows Brown to break his silence is that Jews, for the first time and in great numbers, have broken their silence. And though criticism by non-Jews may be difficult to accept, providing a "kind of moral blank check" to Israel is helpful neither to Palestinians nor to Israelis; speaking the truth should be seen as an act of loyalty rather than disloyalty. Still, Brown warns against demagogic criticism like comparing Israelis to Nazis, as such a comparison denies the reality of the situation.

The problem for Brown is similar to what other Christian theologians refer to, that is, the double standard of Israel as seeming special and thus being criticised for behaving like other nations. Instead of a double standard, Brown suggests a dialectical tension between Israel as special and Israel as normal, thus though its fears of annihilation are understandable in relation to its memory, in its

---

19- Robert McAfee Brown, "Christians in the West Must Confront the Middle East," in Rosemary Radford Ruether and Marc H. Ellis, eds., **Beyond Occupation** (Boston: Beacon, 1990), 139-142. Also see Brown's earlier article "Speaking about Israel; Some Ground Rules," **Christian Century** 105 (6 April 1988): 338-40.

operation as a state in welfare or dealing with refugees, for example, it is to be judged like any other nation. With this in mind Brown makes a plea to Israel: "You, more then all the other peoples of the earth, know what it is like to be refugees, sojourners, displaced persons, people whose lands have been overrun time and again by invaders. Your psalms and liturgies invoke that sense of homelessness as something to be overcome. The Torah calls on you to welcome the sojourner, to feed the hungry, to care for the sick and dying. Could you not exercise that kind concern for the Palestinians 'within your gates' today?"[20]

Brown concludes his essay with a discussion of a possible liberation theology for the Middle East, the elements of which include theological reflection growing out of the immediate situation; a true liberation achieved for all, rather than for some at the expense of others; a preferential option for the poor that leads to the empowerment of the weak, the Palestinians, as well as the now strong Israelis; recognition of the inherent risk in the liberation struggle, that the once-oppressed Jews will continue to oppress and that the oppressed Palestinians, once liberated, may oppress the once more powerful Israelis. The more specific list of ingredients to be part of the solution from Brown's perspective include: a homeland for both Jews and Palestinians;

20- Ibid., 145-146

safeguarding the rights of all minorities; respect for one another borders; bilateral de-escalation of the military forces; a willingness to have all parties judged by the same moral and political standards; an acknowledgment that everyone will have to settle for less than initially hoped for.[21]

Another theologian involved in a reappraisal of the Christian stance is Rosemary Radford Ruether, a Catholic theologian at Garrett Evangelical Seminary in Illinois. Since the publication of her book *Faith and Fratricide* in 1974, Ruether has become well known and respected for her critique of Christian triumphalism as a way of solidarity with the Jewish people. To her, the anti-Judaic bias that has accompanied the history of Christianity lives on in the present, thus continuing to nourish the roots of anti-Jewishness. A vital key for understanding aspects of Western history is therefore lost, and Christian theologians continue to write and to preach theologies that are implicitly, if not explicitly, anti-Jewish. This selective ignorance is then passed on in the churches in a way that continues to reinforce the stereotype of the carnal, legalistic, and obsolete Jew. "This very suppression of Jewish history and experience from Christian consciousness is tacitly genocidal," Ruether writes. "What it says, in effect, is that the Jews have no further right to exist after Jesus. We repress the memory of their

---

21- Ibid., 148-154.

continued existence and our dealings with them so that it appears that 'after Christ' Jews disappear, and only Christians remain as the heirs of Jewish history and the people with a future."[22]

At the same time Christians can not let past history silence them with regard to present abuses, nor can they assert from a Christian viewpoint the obsolete theological right of Israel to exist as a political state. Here Ruether takes on the difficult task for the Christian of speaking truth to Jewish power without being or being considered anti-Jewish. For Ruether, the critical analysis of Jewish suffering in European history must now be complemented by a critical analysis of how one response to that suffering, Zionism, has in the past and present affected the Palestinian people. Second is how Jewish and Christian theology has helped to legitimate Zionism in the past and the present, as well as the need to develop Jewish and Christian theologies that oppose the injustices inherent in Zionist ideology and practice. At the same time, Ruether finds it difficult or impossible for Christians to analyse the historical or theological patterns

---

22-Rosemary Redford Ruether, Faith and Fratricide: The Theological Roots of Anti - Semitism (New York: Seabury, 1974), 258, 225. Ruether, **Faith and Fratricide, 258,225**. Ruether ends her book with a proposal to reform current theological curricula about the Jews. She includes teaching the Jewish scriptures from a Jewish perspective, correcting the stereotypes of the Pharisees and thus the myth of blood guilt, and studying the way theological anti-Jewishness has been translated into social and political oppression (pp. 259-61).

unless and until they come into contact and solidarity with the Palestinian people. Thus comes the crucial question that Brown broached earlier: whether Christians can be in solidarity with Jews and Palestinians.[23]

The answer for Ruether, as for Brown, is yes, but only when the myths of Israelis as innocent and Palestinians as terrorists are exposed. By analysing Zionist and Palestinian history, Ruether concludes that the chief impediment to peace has not been historically and is not today the Palestinian people but an expansionist and violent state of Israel. This impediment to peace lies in the concept of Israel as an exclusive Jewish state and also in Israel's position as an occupying power. Underlying both these realities is the refusal to recognise, alongside Jewish nationalism, a parallel Palestinian nationalism and right to self-determination. Though Ruether believes that a Jewish homeland should be understood as a powerful part of contemporary Jewish identity, this understanding does not on the face of it give Jews a political right to found a state, much less to displace the Palestinian people in the process. Thus for Ruether three myths need to be overcome: that Jews have *a priori* right to the whole of Palestine; that the Arab Palestinians do not have a parallel claim on the

---

23- Rosemary Radford Ruether and Herman Ruether, **The Wrath of Jonah: The Crisis of Religious Nationalism in the Israeli-Palestinian Conflict** (New York: Harper & Row, 1989), xix, 244.

land as a national community; and that Israel must be oriented toward European people and culture and not be part of the Middle East. It is these three Zionist myths that have walled "Israel into a segregated, hostile, and violent relationship to the rest of the communities of people that live around it."[24]

Although Ruether acknowledges that Jews have a fear of annihilation that comes from the Holocaust, it is unfair, she says, to transfer this fear to the Arabs. Palestinians cannot be expected to address this almost pathological fear that Jews have of them, "since it makes little sense to their own experience as refugees and as an oppressed community with no state, little land, no army worth mentioning and so little political clout that only by suffering endless assaults does it keep itself before the attention of the world at all." For Ruether, the struggle to demythologise the innocence of Israel is less an academic question than a struggle for the survival of the Palestinian people. In her most recent essay, "The Occupation Must End," Ruether details the brutal response of Israel to the Palestinian uprising in

---

24- Robert McAfee Brown, "Christians in the West Must Confront the Middle East," in Rosemary Radford Ruether and Marc H. Ellis, eds., **Beyond Occupation** (Boston: Beacon, 1990, 139-142. Also see Brown's earlier article "Speaking about Israel; Some Ground Rules" **Christian Century** 105 (6 April 1988): 145-146

terms of injuries and deaths, now approaching eighty thousand, and the assault on Palestinian culture and education as a way of punishing and humiliating a people.[25]

As might be expected, Ruether finds it difficult to communicate these facts to Christians in the West, because the flip side of anti-Jewishness has become philo-Semitism. This is a tendency to idealise Jews to the point of elevating them to a position of superior wisdom and morality, a tendency particularly true of liberal Christians who harbour an intense guilt for Jewish sufferings, past and present. "When faced with the possibility that an organised group of Jews have done some pretty bad things to another group of people, any sensitive, anti-anti-Semites are thrown into agonised emotional conflict. We fear that we might be slipping back into negative stereotypes of Jews and quickly censor the thought that 'maybe those Jews are bad people after all.' This suggests to me that we Christians, with a history of negative stereotypes of Jews, have a hard time dealing with Jews as complex beings like ourselves."

Christian thinking about Jews therefore swings between two unrealistic polarities - Jews as superior to Christians, paragons of wisdom and moral insight, and Jews as inferior to Christians, untrustworthy and

---

25- Rosemary Radford Ruether, "Beyond Anti-Semitism and Philo-Semitism," in Ruether and Ellis, **Beyond Occupation**, 289.

lacking in true capacity for moral and spiritual life. As Ruether envisions it, the task is to see Jews as different, with their own particular history and culture, and similar, with the same human attributes and propensities as others. Christians are just going to have to face the complexity of human nature in Jews as they learn to face it in themselves: the reality of the Jews in Israel has been of a dominant conquering power displacing another people and seeking to make them disappear.[26]

The challenge for Christians is to see Jews as they are, but the conflict in Israel and Palestine also challenges the Jewish people to move beyond a particularity that emphasises uniqueness in order to justify exclusivity, which in turn seeks to confer a special holiness with rights to the land that supersede the claims of others. Ruether suggests instead that Jews choose the universalist tradition in Judaism, which affirms particularly in solidarity with the particularity of other peoples. This ethic of mutual solidarity does not mean an anonymous universalism that contains (as it did in the past) a hidden agenda of ending Jewish distinctiveness, an agenda Jews rightly resist. "Rather, one must locate it in the concrete relations between different people who are actually called, either by choice or by historical circumstances, to live side by side with each other. The quest of Israeli Jews and Palestinian Arabs for a

---

26- Ibid., 25

just and peaceful coexistence is an instance of the difficulty and challenge of that ethical commandment."

Ultimately, to choose a different path, more than innocence and exclusivism needs to be given up. The understanding of Israel as redemptive is also thrown into question, for religious messianism in Holocaust theology and fundamentalist groups, rather than a healing and unifying force, has become a force of violence within the Jewish community as well as outward toward Palestinians. As Ruether comments:

> The Sabra, redeemed from Diaspora weakness, with a gun in one hand and a plow in the other, has become a military-political-industrial ruling elite. Many Jews no longer work the land with their own hands or do any kind of manual labour. For many, such labour is now seen as "Arab work," unbefitting a Jew. Some Israelis have become an urban managerial elite ruling over lower classes and races who do the manual labour. The dream of redemption through labour has evaporated in the reality of a colonist, capitalist organisation of the economy. The class and race hierarchy of labour, relegation of Palestinians to third-class citizens or

stateless subjects of military rule, also destroys the messianic myth of Israel as model social democracy, a "light to the nations," in terms of democratic and socialist ideals.[27]

27- Ruether & Ruether, **Wrath of Jonah**, 237.

Toward a Jewish-Christian Palestinian solidarity

What Brown and especially Ruether point to from the Christian viewpoint is exactly what is critical from the Jewish side as well: a move beyond the abstraction of Jewish innocence and Israel as redemptive toward a concrete accounting of an occupation which is oppressing another people. The important point here is that Christians are willing to move beyond their own innocence and redemption as well. In fact, the ability to move forward on the question of Israel and Palestine is directly linked to admitting that the Jewish and Christian thought of redemption when played out in the world is a catastrophe for the people who have to suffer it. In short, redemption - the Christian vision that every head should bow before Christ or the Jewish version of the greater and of Israel - is covered with blood.

But as should now be apparent, the pursuit of redemption is not only a burden to be borne, say, by Jews within Christendom and Palestinians within the

Greater Israel - that is a burden to the obvious victims. It also creates victims within the oppressing community. By oppressing others religion becomes a servant of the state and is used to legitimate state power, as is seen most explicitly in the Christian Constantinian synthesis, which originated in the fourth century when Constantine became the first Roman emperor to make Christianity a state religion. It still is in evidence today. From the Christian side, the ecumenical dialogue begins with the knowledge that this synthesis has been a disaster for Christianity itself. Paradoxically, at the same time as Christianity attempts to shed this albatross, it is Judaism which embarks on a Constantinianism of its own. Thus the freeing of Christianty and Christian theology from its dependence on state power sadly is joined by a developing Constantinian Judaism. Of course, within Constantinian religiosity priests and rabbis continue to be produced; the churches and synagogues become even more elaborate. However, the bottom falls out, the ethical witness diminishes, and the discussions about ethical witness contain an emptiness about which everyone knows and agrees to remain silent.

As Brown and Ruether articulate it, the renewal of Christianity comes through identifying its victims, external and internal, and the Jewish victims of Christianity play a tremendous role in this renewal. This is one part of the ecumenical dialogue. But today the renewal of Judaism and the Jewish people can only come through attention to its victims, the Palestinian people. Thus the ecumenical dialogue and the concomitant ecumenical deal come to an end because of the changing nature and objective circumstances of Jews and Christians. Yet with the end of the ecumenical dialogue, Jews and Christians are poised on a new and exciting possibility, that of a Jewish-Christian solidarity based on mutual repentance for sins and a mutual recognition that the redemption of each is at a bloody cost to the "other."

Here the Palestinians are central because they inform Christians that Jews are no longer simply innocent victims, and that Christians participate in a new crime by virtue of their silence. Palestinians are central as well because they embody in their dispersal and destruction the end of the Jewish tradition as we have inherited it. Thus Palestinians call Christians and Jews to an accounting which may lead to a greater maturity of each faith group and a new self-definition, hence a series of new possibilities, including the chance of Christian and Jewish healing.

Perhaps the exploration of what it means to be Jewish beyond Constantinian Judaism rests with a new form of solidarity with Christians and Palestinians that poses the fundamental religious choice before us as a people. Is it possible after the Holocaust to embrace our former enemies,

Christians, and our present "enemies," the Palestinian people? Is it possible after experiencing empire, the Holocaust, and forging empire in the greater land of Israel to once again pursue community, the sharing of land and destiny? Can we be healed of our own trauma if we do not recognise the trauma we are causing to another people? Can we feel safe in a world of domination, can we even ask the question of God after the Holocaust without this pursuit of community? We can hardly ask these questions alone. Is it possible, though, to ask these questions anew with Christians and Palestinians?

So today, after Auschwitz and the Palestinian uprising, the path becomes clear. The future of Christianity in the West is somehow tied to the encounter with the Jewish people in the present and the future of the Jewish people is tied to the preservation and flourishing of Palestine within the Jewish word. In light of this, it is incumbent upon Jewish and Christian progressives to move toward a Jewish-Christian-Palestinian solidarity which recognises both the tragedy of the present and the hope of the future.

I close as I began, with a story. Several years ago I lectured at a conference celebrating the hundredth anniversary of the birth of Eugene Rosenstock-Hussey, a German Jew who had converted to Christianity and who through dialogue challenged Franz Rosenweig, another German Jew, to retain his Jewishness. Since both figures were German, a fairly large percentage of the conference attendees were German. After my talk, I was startled when a German woman, unused to public expressions of grief, took my hand and began to cry. In broken English, her words interrupted by sobs, she repeated over and over again her sorrow for what had happened to Jews and her inability to undo what had been done. As I held her hand, shaken myself, with little to do but to stand with her, another German came up to us and said, "You do not understand what it is for us to hear a Jewish voice." Later that night, trying to make sense of the tears and these parting words, I realised its underlying meaning: history had gone too far, there was no way back and no way to heal because the Jewish presence had been removed forever from Germany. The implications of this encounter for Jews and Palestinians is obvious, and this is what shook me when I was invited to speak on the subject of Sabra and Shatilea. Will Jewish children tomorrow, when meeting and hearing a Palestinian, voice same the regret, utter the same cry, a cry which cannot be satisfied because history has gone too far? Unlike the Germans, the horror has yet to be fully - or irreparably - realised. The hour, though, is very late.

CHAPTER THREE

The renewal of Palestine in the Jewish imagination

In April 1992 I joined with twenty other Jewish scholars and intellectuals from around the word to advise the Polish government on the future of the museum at Auschwitz. Over 600,000 people visit Auschwitz every year and the purpose of our delegation was to help expand the narrative of suffering previously presented to these visitors, emphasising for the first time that over 90% of the people killed at Auschwitz were Jewish.

On the second day, while awaiting the bus that would take us from Krakow to Auschwitz, a startling a news story circulated among the participants: Yassir Arafat's plane was missing in Libya and he was presumed dead. I recall my first thought: "I am at Auschwitz and Arafat is dead." My second thought was the need for silence - perhaps we should all take a moment of silence, for a great leader of Palestine was dead. Faces of the Palestinians I know were before me; I felt for them as individuals and as a people a deep sadness. Yet these thoughts and feelings were internal to me. The discussion revolved around how this event would influence the upcoming Israeli elections. Would the Israeli population veer to the right or the left ? How would Shamir and Rabin use this death to rally their supporters ?

What struck me then, as it does now, is the superficiality of my colleagues, response. Politically these Jewish intellectuals and scholars were "progressive," but their relation to the Palestinian people was totally abstract, or perhaps more accurately stated, simply did not exist. My impulse was to seek to engage them at a deeper level; almost immediately, however, I realised the futility of the effort and the impossibility of connecting. Perhaps, after much discussion they would grant a positive destiny for Palestinians within a small, dependent, demilitarized Palestinian state. Yet in the final analysis, for Jews, Palestinians existed only within a Jewish framework, as those who hinder, obstruct, even terrorize Jews. Thus the sole interpretive framework of the death of Arafat was a chapter in a singularly Jewish drama.

This isolated and circumscribed Jewish interpretive framework is both significant and functional. We came to Auschwitz to demand a narrative which emphasizes an accounting of the crimes against our people, and we had every right to demand that. Since the Palestinians are largely invisible to Jews, they are only occasionally permitted to enter into our consciousness, and then only on our terms, and thus can demand no accounting of us. Auschwitz and Israel, our suffering and our empowerment, serve as a continuous narrative for Jews. A hint of "peoplehood" and nationality, the slightest sense that Arafat is important to people whom we are oppressing - and therefore that Arafat is extremely important to us as Jews, not simply in political terms, but in the larger framework of Jewish history in which we are no longer innocent - in a sense is impossible to affirm. To accord this larger import to Arafat is to recognize Palestinian peoplehood, to move beyond the slogan of a two state solution (with Palestinians confined to 12-15% of the land of Palestine) and envision a renewed, diverse and unitary Palestine as an imperative of Jewish history. To recognize Palestine is to move beyond the sense of Jews as innocent and Israel as redemptive.

But how could we as Jews, with Auschwitz as our anchor of memory, imagine such a Palestine? Two decades earlier, as a student of the Holocaust theologian Richard Rubenstein, I read his groundbreaking *After Auschwitz: Radical Theology and Contemporary Judaism*, which raised profound questions about the Jewish past, and the possibility of human solidarity after the Holocaust. And now I was part of a group investigating the future of Auschwitz. However, with the week over and time for deeper reflection, a phrase kept resonating which at first I hardly understood. That phrase was "ending Auschwitz." I ask: If we dwell only in Auschwitz, in our past suffering, how can we understand suffering in the contemporary world? And if Auschwitz as an anchor of memory is used as a blunt instrument of oppression, how can we understand the suffering of the Palestinian people at our hands? In my reflections I also saw "ending Auschwitz" in a positive context. Perhaps by understanding our contemporary use - and abuse - of power we can recognize the Palestinian people as we longed to be recognized in our past times of travail. Perhaps by recognizing the Palestinian people we can see a choice beyond being victims or oppressors. Could this recognition signal the beginning of a reconciliation with those whom we oppressed and thus lead to a reconciliation with our own past suffering? Could it be that the healing of the Palestinian trauma is absolutely essential for the healing of the Jewish trauma, and that the reintegration of Palestine is as essential to Jewish history as it is to Palestinian history.? And could it be that the only way to finally end Auschwitz is to reimage Palestine where for Jews only an innocent and yet in reality an imperial Israel exists today ?[1]

---

[1] Richard Rubenstein, *After Auschwitz: Radical Theology and Contemporary Judaism* (New York: Bobbs-Merrill, 1966). Rubenstein, who was part of this delegation to Auschwitz, is quite hawkish on the question of Israel. For Rubenstein's latest views on Israel see his critique of my own work in Otto Maduro, ed., *Jews, Christians and Liberation Theology: An Agenda for Dialogue* (Maryknoll: Orbis,1991), 96-109.

An inclusive liturgy of destruction

What my colleagues had forgotten or, if remembered, had repressed, is a long history of Jews recognizing the reality and the implications of Jewish oppression of the Palestinian people. In fact we might say that from the beginning of Zionism and accelerating with the creation of the Israeli state, a vast literature has come into being which understands the Jewish liturgy of destruction as now including the Palestinian people. Though this is unmentioned and often repressed today, with the founding of the state of Israel Jews for the first time began to see the suffering of another people, the Palestinian Arabs, in light of the suffering of the Jewish people.[2]

Examples of this abound. In 1948 Israeli intelligence

2- For a discussion of the Jewish liturgy of destruction, see David G. Roskies, *Against the Apocalypse: Responses to Catastrophe in Modern Jewish Culture* (Cambridge: Harvard University Press, 1984). Roskies was also part of the delegation to Auschwitz and objected to my inclusion of Palestinians in the Jewish liturgy of destruction. Roskies takes seriously his role as a "guardian of the Holocaust."

officer Shamarya Guttman was involved in the occupation of the palestinian Arab Lydda and the subsequent expulsion of its inhabitants. Benny Morris, the Jewish Israeli historian, describes it:

> All the Israelis who witnessed the events agreed that the exodus, under a hot July sun, was an extended episode of suffering for the refugees, especially from Lydda. Some were stripped by soldiers of their valuables as they left town or at checkpoints along the way. Guttman subsequently described the trek of the Lydda refugees: A multitude of inhabitants walked one after another. Women walked burdened with packages and sacks on their heads. Mothers dragged children after them.... Occasionally, warning shots were heard...Occasionally, you encountered a piercing look from one of the youngsters ....in the column, and the look said: 'We have not surrendered. We shall return to fight you.' For Guttman, an archaeologist, the spectacle conjured up the memory of the the exile of Israel {at the end of the Second Commonwealth, at Roman hands.}[3]

3- Benny Morris, *The Birth of the Palestinian Refugee Problem, 1947-1949* (Cambridge University Press, 1987), 210

Morris continues this description:

> One Israeli soldier (probably 3rd Battalion), from Kibbutz Ein Harod, a few weeks after the event recorded vivid impression of the thirst and hunger of the refugees on the roads, and how 'children got lost' and of how a child fell into a well and drowned, ignored, as his fellow refugees fought each other to draw water. Another soldier described the spoor left by the slow-shuffling columns, "to begin with {jettisoning} utensils and furniture and in the end, bodies of men, women and children, scattered along the way." Quite a few refugees died - from exhaustion, dehydration and disease along the roads eastward, from Lydda and Ramle, before reaching temporary rest near and in Ramallah. Nirm al Khatib put the death toll among the Lydda refugees during the trek eastward at 335, Arab Legion commander John Glubb Pasha, more carefully wrote that nobody will ever know how many children died.[4]

In the weeks that followed, a co-leader of the Mapam party, Meir Ya'ari, lamented: " Many of us

---

4- Ibid., 3

are losing their [human] image... How easily they speak of how it is possible and permissible to take women, children and old men and to fill the road with them because such is the imperative of strategy. And this we say, the members of Hashmer Hatzair, who remember who used this means against our people during the Second World] war.. I am appalled."[5]

These and other atrocities and expulsions occasioned some months later a ministerial probe which was discussed in Mapam's executive body. At the start of the meeting Benny Marshak explicitly asked that members refrain from using the phrase "Nazi actions." Later at a cabinet meeting Aharon Cizling, Minister of Agriculture, told the other cabinet member that "I couldn't sleep all night ... This is something that determines the character of the nation.. Jews too have committed Nazi acts."[6]

In all of this something is happening that is both ancient and new. The reference, in a time of crisis, to an ancient Jewish archetype of destruction, the memory of the exile of Israel with the destruction of the Temple by the Romans in 70 A.C.E. and to the Holocaust, are now in relation to the suffering of another people at the hands of Jewish people. This is intuitively understood and even the desire to keep

---

5- Ibid., 211
6- Ibid., .223

this connection from being spoken belied the obvious: that at least some Jews were seeing in the Palestinian people their own history. And in observing that history, in sad and profound ways, they were recognizing that the history of Jews and Palestinians is somehow, in the expulsions and massacres, bound together.

But it is also clear at the very beginning that the ability to see this bond is intimately related to the ability to admit that Jews are no longer innocent, and this is precisely the most controversial issue. Thus many at the outset wanted to change the intuitive language to address procedural matters and long range goals, in a sense to bury the intuitive connection. In their mind any comparison from within or from outside places the legitimacy of Jewish empowerment in question. And, too, it cast doubt on the entire policy of separating the two communities, which gained strength as the war continued and Israel was, to a larger extent, emptied of Palestinians. One cannot help but hear, as these actors saw with their own eyes, the tension between the prophetic - questioning power - with the process of normalization - adjusting for the obvious excess, though continuing the pursuit of the general goal. For those who pursued normalization, the time had come for Jews to grow up and to suppress the ancient and contemporary images of destruction which define a landscape better forgotten.

The Israeli invasion of Lebanon in 1982 also brought forth this intuitive connection between the suffering Jews had experienced and the suffering Jews were now causing. Jacobo Timerman, who had been imprisoned in Argentina and, upon his release, went to Israel, wrote in 1982:

> Yes, we have killed our moral integrity. I feel that quite soon the Diasora Jews will begin to experience the consequences of the process started by Menachem Begin, when they are denied the right to symbolize the pain of this century, the right to represent the universality of the victim. We are victims who have created our own victims in acts of cruelty. From now on, our tragedy will be inseparable from that of the Palestinians. Perhaps some of us will try to side-step the Israeli moral collapse by resorting to statistics and comparing Auschwitz to Beirut. It will be in vain. The victims of Auschwitz would never have bombed Beirut. Our moral collapse cannot be diluted by statistics.[7]

7- Jacob Timerman, *The Longest War: Israel in Lebanon*, trans. Miguel Acoca (New York: Vintage, 1982), 156-157. Timerman writes: Today in Beirut Arab children have their legs and arms amputated by candlelight in the basements of hospitals destroyed by bombs, without anaesthetics, without sterlization. It is eleven days since proud veteran Israeli troops cut the electricity and water, and food and fuel supplies (162).

In August 1982 as Timerman was covering the war as a journalist, a survivor of the Warsaw ghetto and Buchenwald staged a hunger strike against Menachem Begin's policy of bombing the city of Beirut. The protestor's son was an Israeli paratrooper:

> When I was a child of ten and was liberated from the concentration camp, I thought that we shall never suffer again. I did not dream that we would cause suffering to others. Today we are doing just that. The Germans in Buchenwald starved us to death. Today in Jerusalem, I starve myself, and this hunger of mine is no less horrific. When I hear "filthy Arabs" I remember: "filthy Jews." I see Beirut and I remember Warsaw.[8]

Two stories from the Palestinian intifada make this connection of Palestinian and Jewish history in relation to the Holocaust. Just months after the uprising had begun Marcus Levin, a physician, was called up for reserve duty in the Ansar 2 prison camp. When he arrived Levin met two of his colleagues and asked for information as to his duties. The answer: "Mainly you examine prisoners before and after the interrogation." Levin responded in amazement, "After the interrogation?" which

---

8- Quoted in *Ha'aretz*, August 11, 1982.

prompted the reply, "Nothing special, sometimes there are fractures. For instance, yesterday they brought a twelve-year old boy with broken legs." Dr. Levin then demanded a meeting with the compound commander and told him, "My name is Marcus Levin and not Josef Mengele, and for reasons of conscience I refuse to serve in this place." A doctor who was present at the meeting tried to calm Levin with the following comment: "Marcus, first you feel like Mengele, but after a few days you get used to it." Hence the title of an article written about the incident, " You will Get Used to Being a Mengele."[9]

Three years into the intifada, in 1991, Ari Shavit, while performing his annual reserve service as a guard in the internment camp Gaza Beach, offered this reflection:

> And yet the unjust analogy with those other camps of fifty years ago won't go away. It is not suggested by anti-Israel propaganda. It is in the language the soldiers use as a matter of course: when A. gets up to do guard duty in the interrogation section, he says, "I'm off, late for the Inquisition."
>
> When R. sees a line of prisoners approaching under the barrels of his

---
9- Gideon Spiro, " You will Get Used to Being a Mengele, "*Al Hamishar*, September 19, 1988.

friends' M-16s, he says with quiet intensity: "Look. The Aktion has begun."

And N., who has strong right-wing views, grumbles to anyone who will listen that the place resembles a concentration camp.

M., with a thin smile, explains that he has accumulated so many days in reserve duty during the intifada that soon they will promote him to a senior Gestapo official.

And I, too, who have always abhorred this analogy, who have always argued bitterly with anyone who so much as hints at it, I can no longer stop myself. The associations are too strong... .

Like a believer whose faith is cracking, I go over and over again in my heart the long list of arguments, the list of the differences. There are no crematoria here, I remind myself, and there was no conflict between peoples there. Germany, with its racist doctrine, was organised evil, its people were not in danger, and so on.

But then I realised that the problem is not

> in the similarity - for no one can seriously think that there is a real similarity - but that there isn't enough lack of similarity. The problem is that the lack of similarity isn't strong enough to silence once and for all the evil echoes, the accusing images.[10]

The references in these articles to the Nazi physician Mengele and to the concentration camps as a way of seeing contemporary Jewish Israeli policy and activity is startling. What are we to make of these references? First, it is important to see that they are not primarily comparisons between Nazi and Israeli behaviour, though some of the behaviour may in fact be comparable. Secondly, these references are not attempts to further political objectives, such as promoting one political party over another or de-legitimating the state of Israel, though clearly they subvert partisan and bi-partisan policies of Israel which lead to these situations. Rather, the force of the Nazi reference involves and moves beyond comparison and politics and represents an intuitive link between the historic suffering of the Jews and the present suffering of Palestinians. It further represents an implicit recognition that what was done to Jews is now being

---

10- Ari Shavit, "On Gaza Beach," *New York Review of Books* 38 (July 18, 1991): 78. In relation to the taking of Palestine in Jewish History, see Yaron London, "A Lebenstraum for Whom?" *Yediot Ahronot*, February 24, 1992.

done by Jews to other people. At the same time, the connection of Jewish and Palestinian suffering is pre-political and pre-ideogical, that is, it operates in a terrain filled with the images of Jewish suffering that remains untouched by the "realities" of the situation, the need to be "strong" or even the communal penalties for speaking the truth. We might say that the Nazi reference represents a cry of pain and a plea to end a madness which was visited upon Jews for millennia and now is visited by Jews upon another people. Thus the vehemence with which such analogies are met when spoken, almost as if a blunt instrument is needed to repress the memories and aspirations of the Jewish people to be neither victim nor oppressor. Could it be said that it is impossible today to understand the Jewish liturgy of destruction, the burning of the Temple, the death of the martyr and the pogrom, the events of exile and the Holocaust, unless Jews include as intimate partners those whom Jews have expelled, tortured and murdered as well, those who for most Jews exist without names and histories, the Palestinian people? And that here in an inclusive liturgy of destruction lies the possibility and the hope of moving a tradition of dissent beyond the peripheral and the superficial into an engaged struggle - on behalf of the history of the Jewish and Palestinian people? And that this might liberate Jews from policies and attitudes which when understood intuitively are a betrayal of Jewish history, but through argument and circumstance have been seen as weakness, a lack of political maturity, or even self-hate? Is it possible that this could release Jews from theologies, Holocaust and progressive, which now serve as ideologies closing off critical thought and serving the powerful? To pursue this connectedness means a serious reevaluation of parts of Jewish history, but can this painful task be accomplished without the voices and the faces of those who Jews have initiated into the liturgy of destruction? Can Jews see themselves and their history in a new light without hearing and taking seriously the history and the struggle of the Palestinian people?

The failure of Jewish theology

Unfortunately, when one surveys contemporary Jewish theological literature, the intuitive connection found in the inclusive liturgy of destruction is almost completely missing. That is, the ideological framework for understanding and articulating what intuitively is understood is absent, or, to put it more succinctly, this framework actually labels as heretical the intuitive understandings and their articulation.

Recent Jewish theological writing is noticeably devoid of Palestinians, and when they are mentioned at all it is almost exclusively within a Jewish framework. For example, in Emil Fackenheim's *What is Judaism? An Interpretation for the Present Age*, his first book after moving to Israel, he does not mention Palestinians once. In a massive compilation of essays on critical concepts, movements and beliefs in Jewish life edited by the late Arthur Cohen and Paul Mendes-Flohr, titled *Contemporary Jewish*

Religious Thought, in 1076 pages Palestinians are mentioned less than five times. And when the Nobel laureate Elie Wiesel and Orthodox rabbi Irving Greenberg, both prominent Holocaust theologians, do mention Palestinians, they exist primarily within the Jewish framework of interpretation. As Greenberg writes in a tone typical of Jewish writing, even when partially sympathetic to Palestinian aspirations, "Ideally, the Palestinians should earn their way - all the way to statehood - by peaceful behaviour and policies." Or more to the point, "The Palestinians will have to earn their power by living peacefully and convincing Israel of their beneficence or by acquiescing to a situation in which Israel's strength guarantees that the Arabs cannot use their power to endanger Israel." By banishing Palestinians from the internal landscape of Jewish history, Israel remains essentially innocent. But from a Palestinian perspective who is in need of protection, Israelis or Palestinians? And who, with the experience of the last twenty-five years, on balance, needs assurance?[11]

Wiesel's most extensive discussion of Palestinian issues occurs in 1978 and 1988, and is important to analyse because of his power within the Jewish community and his ability to articulate mainstream

---

11- Irving Greenberg, "The Third Great Cycle in Jewish History," *Perspectives* (New York: National Jewish Resource Center, 1981), 25, 26. See also Emil Fackenheim, *What is Judaism: An Interpretation for the Present Age* (New York: Summit Books, 1987) and Arthur A. Cohen and Paul Mendes-Flohr, eds., *Contemporary Jewish Religious Thought* (New York: Free Press, 1987).

Jewish understanding. His first discussion occurs in the form of a letter "To a Young Palestinian Arab." Wiesel begins his letter with an outstretched hand, promising sincerity which is the only path for those who have suffered. Facing that pain, Wiesel plans to "judge myself as well, since someone else's suffering always puts us to the test." In order to engage in a dialogue, Wiesel counsels putting aside politics as a confusing and superficial labyrinth. To be sure, the arguments on both sides are valid; the Palestinians can invoke Palestine's Moslem past as Wiesel can speak of the Jewish past which preceded it. The injustices endured by Arab refugees in 1948 can also be countered by the Jewish suffering in the Holocaust. But the injustice endured by the Arabs is for Wiesel the responsibility of the Arabs themselves: "Your own leaders, with their incendiary speeches, their virulent fanaticism. If only they had accepted the United Nations' resolutions on the partition of Palestine, if only they had not incited the Arab population to mass flight in order to return 'forthwith' as victors; if only they had not attempted to drown the young Jewish nation in blood; if only they had taken into account Jewish suffering also, the Jewish right to also claim its sovereignty on its ancestral land...For thirty years Israel's peace initiatives were ignored; Israel's appeals for mutual recognition were denied; Israel's conciliatory moves were rejected."[12]

12- Elie Wiesel, *A Jew Today* (New York: Vintage, 1978), 121, 122.

The renewal of Palestine in the Jewish imagination

As for the Jews who emerged "from the darkest recess of history, from the most hidden marshes of man's and God's imagination" they chose to "opt for man" rather than vengeance. For Wiesel, those who went to Palestine did so to relive an ancient dream together with the Palestinian people, not to displace them. What then divided Wiesel and his Palestinian brother? The use of suffering against others: "Ask your elders and mine; they will tell you that in the immediate postwar years in Europe - in Germany, Hungary, Poland and elsewhere - there were countless collaborators who had every reason to be afraid. But they were not harmed - not by us. And those neighbours of ours who had been present at our agony and had pillaged our homes, sometimes before our eyes, went on living and drinking and sleeping as though nothing had happened. We could have lashed out against them - we did not. We consistently evoked our trials only to remind man of his need to be human - not of his right to punish. On behalf of the dead, we sought consolation, not retribution." Whereas the Palestinian Arabs had done the opposite. While Wiesel felt responsible for what happened to Palestinians, he can not abide by what Palestinians had done with their anger:

> I feel responsible for your sorrow, but not for the way you use it, for in its name you have massacred innocent people, slaughtered children. From Munich to

Maalot, from Lod to Entebbe, from highjacking to highjacking, from ambush to ambush, you have spread terror among unarmed civilians and thrown into mourning families already too often visited by death. You will tell me that all these acts have been the work of your extremist comrades, not yours; but they acted on your behalf, with your approval, since you did not raise your voice to reason with them. You will tell me that it is your tragedy which incited them to murder. By murdering, they debased that tragedy, they betrayed it. Suffering is often unjust, but it never justifies murder.[13]

Here is a simple and crucial error in logic which is almost systemic in Jewish analysis when Palestinians, even as supposedly addressed in a letter, are essentially absent. For the Palestinians the crucial connection in this story is not how Jews reacted in Europe to their former conquerors, but how they acted as they became conquerors in Palestine and Israel. Wiesel's desire to move

---

13- Ibid., 126, 127. Also see Wiesel's letter "To a Brother in Israel" in ibid., 129-137. The letter revolves almost completely around the question of why a Jewish diaspora continues when there is a Jewish state. Unfortunately, Palestinians are referred to only once in passing. That Jews have created a Palestinian diaspora is unmentioned.

beyond the confusion of politics is easily stated when the configuration supports your empowerment. But a Palestinian might respond that a face to face discussion can only take place in an authentic way if the political situation is changed. Therefore without politics the Palestinian is consigned to Jewish turf. But implicit is Wiesel's condemnation of the political and sometimes bitter struggle of a displaced people as vengeful. The Palestinians might reverse Wiesel's framework and speak about a highly organised terrorism against the Palestinian people.

In June 1988, a decade after his initial letter and after months of virtual silence regarding the Palestinian uprising, Elie Wiesel wrote an op-ed piece for the New York Times. Several months earlier he had written a short note commemorating the Warsaw Ghetto uprising.

The following paragraph from that earlier piece contains a veiled reference to the current situation: "Little did we know that in our own lifetime, pseudo-scholars would write books to deny that the greatest of Jewish tragedies ever took place. And that the Jewishness of the Jewish victims would be watered down and cheapened. And that the uniqueness of the Holocaust would be questioned. And that anti-Semitism would be clothed in anti-Zionism. And that vicious minds would dare to compare the state of Israel to Nazi Germany." His article "A Mideast Peace - Is it Impossible?" was his first official statement on the uprising, and told the story of his first trip to Israel since the uprising had begun.[14]

Wiesel records the Israeli military presence in Gaza and the "implacable plight of the tens of thousands of refugees who dwell in inhuman conditions nearby. Their suffering could be sensed everywhere, as if it had a life of its own." He spoke to Palestinians, whose aspirations were a Palestinian state, and to Jewish Israeli soldiers about the possibility of reconciling the needs of security with Judaism's concept of humanism. In the soldiers Wiesel finds determination and sadness, hatred and sorrow. The televised images of the beating of prisoners, breaking of bones and demolition of houses have taken their toll and in the world's eye Israel is taking the place of "America during Vietnam, France during Algeria and the Soviet Union during the Gulag." Unfortunately, from Wiesel's perspective many of these critics are being outdone by "some Jewish intellectuals who had never done anything for Israel but now shamelessly used their Jewishness to justify their attacks against Israel." For Wiesel, criticism of Israel is justified but it often goes beyond the boundaries of the acceptable: "Israel is being presented as mostly blood-thirsty - and that is simply not true. In certain

---

14- Eie Wiesel, "Let Us Remember, Let Us Remember," *New York Times*, April 1, 1988; Ibid., "A Mideast Peace - Is It Possible?" *New York Times*, June 23, 1988.

pro-Arab circles, the argument is even more vicious and ugly: Israel is being compared to Hitler's Germany, its policy to Nazism and the Palestinians of today to the Jews of yesterday. How are we to convince Israel's political adversaries that the Holocaust is beyond politics and beyond analogies?"[15]

Wiesel understands the anger of Palestinians who have been denied self-determination and laments the fact that the territories had been "imposed on Israel in war." Contrary to opinions expressed by others, Wiesel feels that Israel has not lost its soul and its soldiers are not sadists, but a realistic solution-Israeli security and Palestinian self determination - escapes him. Right wing fanatics who speak of transferring Palestinians to Jordan are to Wiesel's mind a disgrace, but, the liberals ready to give up all the territories immediately, to whom are they going to give them? "As long as the P.L.O. remains a terrorist organisation, as long as it has not given up on its goal of destroying Israel, why should Israel negotiate with its leaders? But then, if the P.L.O. is not an interlocutor, who could be? There must be, and are, moderate Palestinians. But many have been assassinated - not by Israelis." Wiesel concludes with a hope which harkens back to his visit to Jerusalem after the 1967 War: "And yet, one must not lose hope. Somehow there must be a solution,

---

15- Wiesel, "Peace."

acceptable to both sides, that would end a tragedy that generates such hatred. If extremists in both camps gain ground, all will suffer. I think of the Arab children whom I watched walking to school-and of the young Jewish soldiers with their tormented gaze. How long will joy be denied to all of them? More than ever, I would like to believe in miracles."[16]

Rabbi Arthur Hertzberg, an American establishment progressive Zionist, responded to Wiesel's essay in an open letter. His response is important as an example of the limits of progressive Jewish thought even as it seeks to critique mainstream Jewish theology. As are many others, Hertzberg is deeply troubled by the cycle of violence among Israelis and Palestinians, at the same time being sympathetic to Palestinian aspirations of self determination. Hertzberg agrees with Wiesel's appeal to Palestinians to halt the throwing of stones and start negotiations. But Hertzberg is astonished that Wiesel does not accompany such an assertion with an appeal to the Israelis to do anything at all - in particular to move away from the policy of repression and toward negotiation.[17]

For Hertzberg the effect of what Wiesel is saying is to support the Likud line, that there are no other

---
16- Ibid., 15
17- Arthur Hertzberg, "An Open Letter to Elie Wiesel ," *New York Review of Books* 35 (August 18, 1988) : 13.

options other than the present course. The discussion of Palestinian extremists, for example, so often cited by Likud and by Wiesel, ignores Jewish extremists who feel commanded to expel Muslims and Christians from Israel. "That a former chief of staff, Rafael Eitan, called the Palestinians 'drugged cockroaches' has, surely, not escaped you attention. I wonder whether you, and I, would have been silent if a Russian general had uttered a comparable slur about Jews demonstrating in Red Square. You know that the prime minister of Israel, Yitzhak Shamir, has been saying that he will not return a singe inch of the West Bank to Arab sovereignty; he has thus stalled even the beginnings of negotiation." And this is true with Jewish dissidents as well. Wiesel's predilection is to accuse Jewish dissenters of endangering Jewish support of Israel, of using their Jewishness to defame Israel.[18]

To Wiesel's question of what Israel and the Jewish people are to do, Hertzberg's response is clear: accept the principle and agree that Palestinians have a right to a territorial base for their national life. But to accept this principle and act upon it, Wiesel has to make a choice which represents an unequivocal break with the Likud party line and to accept the command to act justly, especially when "actions seem imprudent and embarrassing, and never to be silent, even to protect Jewish unity." In

---

18- Ibid., 13

short, Hertzberg calls on Wiesel to re-embrace the prophetic tradition with regard to Israel as he has so eloquently done with the Holocaust. To give aid to the "armed Zealots" in Israel today, even through silence, is to lead to disaster, as it has done in the past in Jewish history. Hertzberg concludes his letter with a plea to move beyond the illusion of Jewish unity and to speak prophetically:

> I keep thinking these days of the saying that both of us have quoted many times, and sometimes at each other, especially in those early years when we were closest. Menachem Mendel of Kotsk, the tortured Hasid of the last century, once said that when the Evil One wants to destroy us, he tempts us through our most virtuous inclinations; we do good deeds at the wrong time, with the wrong intensity, and in a setting in which they do devastating harm. I fear that for all your love of Israel, you, in what you say, sometimes risk falling into the moral trap that Menachem Mendel described. You belong among those who speak the truth, even to Jewish power, and who do not look away because of real or invented Jewish weakness. We show the truest love of Israel and the Jewish people when we remind ourselves that, in

strength or in weakness, we survive not by prudence and not by power, but through justice.[19]

19- Ibid., p. 14. For his other essays relating to the uprising, see Arthur Hertzberg, "The Uprising," *New York Review of Books* 35 (February 4, 1988): 32; "The Turning Point," ibid. 35 (October 13,1988): 60 Also see his essay "The Illusion of Jewish Unity," ibid. 35 (June 16, 1988) and "The Impasse Over Israel," ibid. 37 (October 25, 1990): 41. For an American Christian response to Wiesel see Kathleen Christison, "Is Yours a Selective Memory?" *Washington Report on Middle East Affairs* 10 (March 1991): 29-30.

Palestine before Israel:
A dangerous memory for the future

Hertzberg's discussion with Wiesel is instructive. At one level it involves a dispute, chastising Wiesel for his unwillingness to openly critique the Israeli government. However, on a deeper level there is basic agreement. What should be done is what is best for Jews and Israel. Hertzberg, representing the critique of progressive Jews to the more mainstream Wiesel, points to the limitations of Jewish progressive thought: a self-involved Jewish drama which involves the reclaiming of Jewish innocence and ethics and only peripherally involves Palestinians. In this context the distance between mainstream and progressive Jewish thought should be seen as exaggerated, albeit an exaggeration which has important ramifications. For example, Michael Lerner's *Tikkun*, which carries forth the progressive Jewish religious consensus of Arthur Hertzberg in the intifada, post-Iraqi war world, and in which Palestinians have sometimes placed great hope, remains within an emotional, diverse Jewish debate about the future of Jews, Judaism and the state of Israel. Lerner's consensus position is also laced with a dangerous proviso: any Jew, or Palestinian for that matter, who ventures outside the limits of acceptable discussion is labelled a heretic and excommunicated from the discourse on the future of Israel/Palestine. Thus Palestinians are now welcome to a public discussion on their future as long as they recognise that the future of Israel and the Jewish people takes priority. Palestinians can speak within the context of the Jewish narrative as long as they do not mistake it for their own.[20]

If the anaytical and theological framework is deficient in outlook and supresses the pre-political and pre-theological inclusive liturgy of destruction the liturgy itself is also flawed. The theological narrative is self-involved, revolving around Jewish innocence and redemption. It assumes Jews and Israel as the only important actors and thus the only possible future; the more inclusive narrative functions as a warning of transgression, challenging innocence and redemption with concrete acts of excessive power. Yet the memory activated regards the Palestinians, in their suffering, as reminders, objects, if you will, to call Jews back to historically grounded ethical principles. Palestinians are less subjects in and of themselves than they are anonymous masses providing the background for the drama of Jewish empowerment. Perhaps this is

---

20- A sampling of the progressive Jewish consensus can be found in Michael Lerner, ed., *Tikkun: An Anthology* (Oakland: Tikkun Books, 1992). A good example of the establishment of "Jewish turf" and its arrogance is seen in Lerner's interview with Faisal Husseini in ibid., 358-364.

unavoidable within the narrative framework which even the inclusive liturgy of destruction accepts, that is, the necessity of founding and sustaining the state of Israel. Thus the inclusive liturgy of destruction functions, like Jewish theology, as a witness to the creation of the state and intuitively struggles with its less salient aspects.[21]

However, already missing in the narrative in 1947-1948 and totally absent in the 1990's is the world which was Palestine, a world which could challenge the creation and reality of Israel on its own terms. With the absence of Palestine, Palestinians are seen as either helpless or violent refugees, individuals that one pities or fears - but always in the shadow of the more important Jewish action. This is the reason that the discourse of Jewish and Palestinian claims has narrowed considerably over the last 60 years for both parties and why the present round of peace talks represent a victory for Israel and a defeat for Palestinians, despite much of the rhetoric to the contrary.

Palestine is absent; even Jerusalem as a discussion point is forbidden, and the parameters of this discussion, with some nuanced differences, are accepted by mainstream and progressive Jewish thinkers. The argument is reduced to an autonomy

---

21- For an extended discussion of this inclusive liturgy of destruction see Marc H. Ellis, *Beyond Innocence and Redemption: Confronting the Holocaust and Israeli Power* (San Francisco: Harper Collins, 1990): 96-133.

which would formally ghettoise Palestinian presence in Palestine.[22]

But the Jewish discussion of Palestine, and thus Palestine in the Jewish imagination, was somewhat different when counterbalancing powers were visible and involved. That is to say, the contours of the Jewish presence in Palestine were articulated differently before the triumph of state power in Israel, partially because victory seemed less sure and thus the cost of victory and defeat seemed more tangible.

One might sat that some of the early bi-nationalist Zionists on the ground in Palestine controlled by the British and peopled in the majority by Palestinian Arabs had a sense of perspective and a depth of questioning lost in the conquest of Palestine. Could, then, this view of bi-nationalist Zionists, in the decades before the establishment of the state of Israel, with their admittedly European colonialist mentality toward the Palestinian population and their imposition of a growing Jewish population in Palestine, still speak to the reemergence of a Palestine in the Jewish imagination which moves beyond an imperial Israeli landscape and narrative? Could recalling the Jewish need to negotiate desire and power with friend and foe in pre-Israel Palestine

---

22- This is my argument in "More Setters, No Settlement," *Fortnight* no. 303 (February 1992): 9. My title was "Autonomy and the End of Palestine."

lead to a contemporary Jewish understanding that a counter power is absolutely necessary to reign in an Israeli expansion which threatens to devour everything in its path, including its own citizens and tradition? And could the need to negotiate one day lead to a desire to negotiate and to a crystallisation of exactly what Jews really wanted and want today in a land once called Palestine? With all its difficulties and possibilities, one thing is certain: it is crucial to explore the complexities of a movement which for the last time in contemporary Jewish history functioned within the context of a diverse and unitary Palestine.[23]

An example of one such Jewish bi-nationalist is the American-born Judah Magnes (1877-1948), a Reform rabbi who settled in Jerusalem in 1922 and became the first president of Hebrew University. Magnes' dream, one he shared with other bi-nationalists such as Martin Buber and Hannah Arendt, was to create a Jewish cultural, educational and spiritual center in Palestine to help provide a focus for the world-wide Jewish community in the modern period. Yet he quickly became aware of

---

23- For an extended discussion of the Jewish bi-nationalist idea in Palestine see Susan Lee Hattis, *The Bi-National Idea in Palestine During Mandatory Times* (Haifa: Shikmona, 1970). It is important to note that even those who abandoned the bi-nationalist idea did so from a solely Jewish perspective. See Hans Kohn's letter to Berthold Feiwel and copied to Martin Buber written in Jerusalem on November 21, 1929 in Paul Mendes-Flohr, ed., *A Land of Two Peoples: Martin Buber on Jews and Arabs* (Oxford: Oxford University Press, 1983), 97-100.

forces in the Jewish world which sought to divert that center with a policy of domination and statehood. In a letter to Chaim Weizmann, the influential Zionist leader, dated September 7, 1929, Magnes wrote of the options before the Jewish people in Palestine:

> I think that the time has come when the Jewish policy as to Palestine must be very clear, and that now only one of two policies is possible. Either the logical policy outlined by Jabotinsky in a letter in the Times which came today, basing our Jewish life in Palestine on militarism and imperialism; or a pacific policy that treats as entirely secondary such things as a "Jewish State" or a Jewish majority, or even "The Jewish National Home," and as primary the development of a Jewish spiritual, educational, moral and religious center in Palestine. The first policy has to deal primarily with politics, governments, declarations, propaganda and bayonets, and only secondarily with the Jews, and last of all with the Arabs; whereas the pacific policy has to deal first of all with the Jews, and then with the Arabs, and only incidentally with governments and all the rest.
>
> The imperialist, military and political

policy is based upon mass immigration of Jews and the creation (forcibly if necessary) of a Jewish majority, no matter how much this oppresses the Arabs meanwhile, or deprives them of their rights. In this kind of policy the end always justifies the means. The policy, on the other hand, of developing a Jewish spiritual center does not depend upon mass immigration, or upon depriving the Arabs (or the Jews) of their political rights for a generation or a day; but on the contrary, is desirous of having Palestine become a country of two nations and three religions, all of them having equal rights and none of them having special privileges; a country where nationalism is but the basis of internationalism, where the population is pacifistic and disarmed - in short, the Holy Land. [24]

Magnes saw the difficulties of achieving his own desire that a Jewish spiritual and moral center develop in Palestine. Like other bi-national Zionists - Martin Buber comes to mind - Magnes had a colonial attitude toward Palestinian Arabs, whom he saw as "unhappily still half-savage" with their leaders "almost all small men." Magnes combined

---

24- Arthur A. Goren, ed., *Dissenter in Zion: From the Writings of Judah L. Magnes* (Cambridge: Harvard University Press, 1982), 276.

this perspective with a respect for the same people he derided, as we shall see in his plan for a compromise settlement on Palestine. Regardless, the question remained for Jews:

> The question is do we want to conquer Palestine now as Joshua did in his day - with fire and sword? Or do we want to take cognizance of Jewish religious developments since Joshua - our Prophets, Psalmists and Rabbis, and repeat the words: "Not by might, and not by violence, but by my spirit saith the Lord." The question is, can any country be entered, colonised, and built up pacifistically, and can we Jews do that in the Holy Land? If we can not (and I do not say that we can rise to these heights), I for my part have lost half my interest in the enterprise. If we can not even attempt this, I should much rather see this eternal people without such a "National Home," with the wanderer's staff in hand and forming new ghettos among the peoples of the world.[25]

The following week Magnes wrote to Felix Warburg, an American Jewish banker, philanthropist and community leader, about recent disturbances in

---
25- Ibid., 276.

Jerusalem. Again Magnes combines condescension toward Palestinian Arabs and a critique of Jewish power:

> I must say that I have been amazed that not one official Jewish voice had been lifted in sympathy with such slain and injured Moslems or Christians who may have been innocent; that no money was earmarked for their injured. Of course, the Arabs were the aggressors and the most bloodthirsty. Do I also have to be shouting that? But do you not know that we, too, have had our preachers of hate and disseminators of lies, our armed youth, our provocative processions, our unforgivable stupidity in our handling of the Western Wall incidents since last Yom Kippur, making out what should have been a police incident an international political issue? Politics, statesmanship, hobnobbing with the masters of empire, singing high-sounding phrases instead of disciplining and purifying our community and trying to understand and make terms with our neighbours. [26]

Magnes then outlines his own framework for a settlement of the dispute between Jew and Arab. He begins with the understanding that Palestine does not

---
26- Ibid., 276.

belong to Jew or Arab, or even the three monotheistic religions on an exclusive basis. For Magnes, if Palestine is to truly be the Holy Land, it will have to belong to all of them.

> We must once and for all give up the idea of a "Jewish Palestine" in the sense that a Jewish Palestine is to exclude and do away with an Arab Palestine. This is the historic fact, and Palestine is nothing if it is not history. If a Jewish national home in Palestine is compatible with an Arab national home there, well and good, but if it is not, the name makes very little difference.
>
> The fact is that nothing there is possible unless Jews and Arabs work together in peace for the benefit of their common Holy Land. It must be our endeavour first to convince ourselves and then to convince others that Jews and Arabs, Moslems, Christians, and Jews have each as much right there, no more or less, than the other: equal rights and equal privileges and equal duties. That is practically quite sufficient for all purposes of the Jewish religion, and it is the sole ethical basis of our claims there. Judaism did not begin with Zionism, and if Zionism is ethically not in accord with

Judaism, so much the worse for Zionism.[27]

Years later, in the January 1943 issue of *Foreign Affairs,* Magnes published an essay "Toward Peace in Palestine" which details how this vision of a diverse and unitary Palestine might be preserved. It is important to note that Magnes was by now quite aware of the Nazi atrocities being committed in Europe. Thus Magnes argued for increased Jewish immigration to Palestine within the context of the emergency situation facing European Jews. Still for Magnes the context of European Jewry had to be understood within the context of a land which, far from empty, was home to Palestinian Arabs.[28]

Magnes begins his article by linking the solution of the Jewish problem to the labour of Jews and non-Jews for a free and just society. To those Jews who seek to separate politics and religion or impose messianic religious ideas on the political reality in Palestine, Magnes is firm: "The fact remains that Palestine is small and not empty. Another people have been in possession for centuries, and the concept of Palestine as a Jewish state is regarded by many Arabs as equivalent to a declaration of war against them. To those who contend that Palestine is the promised land of the Jews, I would say that it is

---

27- Ibid. An extended analysis of these views can be found in J.L.Magnes, *Like All The Nations?* (Jerusalem, 1930).
28- Ibid., 389-398.

necessary to distinguish between messianic expectations and hard reality."[29]

To Magnes the conception of Palestine as a Jewish or Arab state leaves little room for compromise and further oppresses the "ordinary" Jew and Arab who have "no hatred for one another and who will rejoice over the prospect of a reasonable settlement which might enable them to live together and to develop their common country in peace." Magnes explicitly rejects the Jewish and Arab proposals of population transfer and calls instead for a Union of Palestine, worked out at a first level by Jews and Arabs and guaranteed by the emerging American power, which is "greatly trusted, having no territorial or imperialistic ambitions here."

Magnes outlines this Union of Palestine under three aspects:

1. Union between Jews and Arabs within a bi-national Palestine

2. Union of Palestine, Transjordan, Syria and Lebanon in an economic and political confederation. These lands form a geographic unit and constituted a poitical and economic union at several times between ancient semitic days and the First World War.

---

[29]- Ibid. An extended analysis of these views can be found in J.L.Magnes, *Like All The Nations?* (Jerusalem, 1930), 389-390

3. Union of this federation with an Anglo-American union which is assumed to be part of that greater union of the free nations now labouring to be born out of the ruins of the decaying world.[30]

Some of the details of this bi-national Palestine envisioned by Magnes are important to the question of the renewal of Palestine in the Jewish imagination. To begin with, a bi-national Palestine "must provide constitutionally for equal rights and duties for both the Jewish and the Arab nations, regardless of which is the majority and which the minority." Political equality should grow from a "bi-national administration, so that officials may be trained as soon as possible for the great tasks which confront them." According to Magnes, the British have failed to train Jews and Palestinian Arabs for the tasks they will soon inherit: "The time has come to put Palestinians, both Jews and Arabs, in charge of non-controversial government departments and to make them members of the Executive Council of Government." As for immigration of Jews to Palestine, a pressing matter as the European catastrophe mounted, Magnes agreed that whatever the yearly immigration allotment, the Jewish population should never be permitted to become more than one-half of the population of Palestine.[31]

30- Ibid. An extended analysis of these views can be found in J.L.Magnes, *Like All The Nations*? (Jerusalem, 1930),393.

As part of the Jewish-Arab compromise, Magnes envisioned Jerusalem as the federal headquarters or capital of Palestine. As the Holy City of three religions, Magnes saw Jerusalem as once again assuming its destiny as a center of spiritual and intellectual exchange. If the three faiths had failed to create societies of righteousness and mercy, the "new Jerusalem, then, would symbolise a new relationship between Judaism, Christianity and Islam in their cradle of origin; and in the New Jerusalem they would work out together part of their common problems with the old-new East which contains among its other elements the vast, vibrating, spiritual powers of Russia, India and China."[32]

Though a rabbi and a thinker, Magnes was also an activist, and he spent his last years lobbying to rescue Palestine from partition and Israeli statehood. Indeed on May 5 and 6, 1948, just months before his death in October and at a critical moment in the 1948 war, Magnes spoke at length with Secretary of State George Marshall and President Harry Truman, suggesting that the United States government withhold recognition from a declaration of Israeli statehood and establish an American trusteeship to provide an umbrella for an eventual bi-national political settlement. This trusteeship would permit a

---
31- Ibid., 393-394
32- Ibid., p.397. Also see M. Buber, J.L.Magnes and E. Simon, eds., *Towards Union In Palestine: Essays on Zionism and Jewish-Arab Cooperation* (Jerusalem:IHUD, 1947).

variety of political options with the central purpose of holding Palestine together as an "integral land." In Magnes' view, under trusteeship there could be a Jewish province, canton, or state, or an Arab province, canton or state, but they would be held together in a federal union. The importance of the trusteeship was obvious to Magnes and was received with interest by both Marshall and Truman because it would allow Jews and Palestinian Arabs to work out, in Truman's words, their "own salvation." Unafraid to suggest means by which this goal could be reached, Magnes proposed to Marshall that the U.S. impose financial sanctions against both the Jews and Arabs in Palestine, and support the dispatch of a special UN representative to organise the Jewish and Arab municipal police to secure Jerusalem.[33]

Magnes - and by extension the bi-nationalist Zionist tradition - is important to recall both for his weaknesses and strengths. When thought of in mainstream and progressive Jewish circles, the weakness of Magnes and the bi-national Zionists is

---

33- Ibid., pp.492, 493. In June 1948 Magnes responded to the unfolding developments in the Middle East which included the declaration of Israeli statehood, by drafting a detailed plan titled "United States of Palestine - A Confederation of Two Independent States." Here he outlined the structures of a political union with particular reference to foreign affairs, defense, international loans, federal courts, and the protection of religious shrines, historical monuments and collections of cultural, artistic and scientific importance. Interestingly enough, this plan was published in the October 1948 issue of *Commentary* as a response to Major Abba Eban's article in the September *Commentary* criticising the discussion of Palestine as put forth by bi-nationalists.

usually seen to be an idealism about the willingness of Palestinian Arabs to share the land with Jews. That is, the weakness, idealism, is used to buttress the views of the necessity of a powerful Israeli state and its innocence. In this scenario, the original sin is the Palestinian Arab rejection of partition which leads to the reluctant militarisation of Jewish life in Israel. From the perspective analysed here, Magnes' weakness is seen in more fundamental areas. At the outset he unilaterally accepts the concept of a Jewish homeland as inherently important for Jews *and* Palestinian Arabs, if the latter will only come to their senses. The Palestinian Arabs are seen through a Western lens, found wanting, and encouraged to grow into this more "mature" sensibility. Thus with Jewish assistance Palestine, perhaps even the whole of the Middle East, can become "productive" again. The infusion of scientific, technological, agricultural and financial means is important to this development and Jews can be the conduit for these advances. Clearly Magnes is naive about the neutrality of American power and even in opposing a military policy he underestimates the ferocity of Jewish

---

33- Of course, Abba Eban was at this moment taking his place as the authentic and progressive Jewish spokesperson on the issue of Israel and the Middle East, a place he has reserved until the present. By the time this letter to the editor was published, Magnes had died and the U.N. representative for whom Magnes had argued, Counte Bernadotte, had been assassinated by Jewish terrorists. Magnes praised Bernadotte as the person "who had come closer than any other man to bringing Jews and Arabs to an understanding," and lamented his murder "as a tragedy of historical importance for both peoples." See Ibid., 511-518.

power once established in the Israeli state. It must be also pointed out that Magnes' aguments were not always stated in complete honesty, a flaw that plagues the authenticity of Jewish progressive thought today. For Magnes, Western Jewish abilities would assure more than an equal pace in a bi-national Palestine; they would eventually win over the Arabs to allow a dominant Jewish role.[34]

Despite these weaknesses, Magnes' strengths are also important. Because he was attempting to justify an insurgent power to a Palestinian and Arab world, Magnes recognised the need to justify and limit this insurgency so as to insure acceptance by the indigenous population and its leaders. And though his vision of a bi-national Palestine was perhaps inevitably skewed toward the West, Magnes realised that Palestine was located in the Middle East and that the future of Jews in Palestine was there, rather than in the Western outpost Israel has become. Hence his plan, unheard of today in Jewish circles,

---

[34]- With regard to a western colonial vision Martin Buber can also be cited. See Buber's letter to Gandhi written from Jerusalem on February 24, 1939 in which he argues that what appears to be a colonial venture really is not one. To prove this point Buber cites the lack of productivity in Arab agriculture compared to Jewish productivity. Buber writes: Ask the soil what the Arabs have done for her in 1300 years and what we have done for her in 50! Would her answer not be weighty testimony in a just discussion as to whom this land "belongs ?" See Mendes-Flohr, ed., *A Land of Two Peoples*, 122. Obviously Magnes, Buber and Arendt were participating in what Edward Said has termed Orientalism, an issue that deserves serious analysis. See Edward Said, *Orientalism* (New York : Random House, 1978).

of federation with other Arab countries and his ability to see the future of the Jewish national home in the larger Arab context.

Magnes truly feared the military conquest for Jews and Arabs, fought it in words and ideas and even lobbied a third power to prevent it. Thus if we can say that Magnes showed a typical Western presumption vis-a-vis peoples of the East, he did in fact draw a line. And finally Magnes envisioned a future Palestine with Jews and Arabs living and working together as two peoples with a constitution guaranteeing their civil rights and equality under law. Though this seems a rational plan within the context of Magnes' vision, it is today revolutionary when compared to the vision put forth by progressive Jews who seek only to distance themselves from a truncated and dependent Palestinian state or autonomous entity.

Palestine and the Jewish future

With the establishment of Israel in 1948, Palestine in the mainstream Jewish imagination was reduced to a problem of refugees to be settled in the larger Arab world. With the fall of Jerusalem, the West Bank and Gaza in June 1967, Palestine assumed a different problematic in the Jewish imagination, that of administering occupied territories and monitoring disturbing demographic potentialities. Indeed, the victories of 1948 and 1967 occasioned celebrations among Jews around the world as a will to survival and the possibility of Jewish empowerment. However, unlike Judah Magnes, little thought was given to the consequences of these victories, either for Palestine and Palestinian history, Palestinian Arabs and Palestinian Arab history or for Jews and Jewish history. The unification of Jerusalem under Jewish control in 1967 points this out vividly. One need only reflect on the differences between Magnes' vision of a shared Jerusalem in a unified Palestine, held together if necessary by outside military power, and the celebratory, almost mystical vision of a Jewish-conquered Jerusalem by Elie Wiesel almost two decades later. What Wiesel and other Holocaust theologians failed to account for was the cost of Jewish empowerment, again for

The renewal of Palestine in the Jewish imagination

Palestinian Arabs and also for Jews. In essence the 1967 war sealed what had begun in 1948: the end of Palestine and the rise of an imperial Israel. The praises sung in Jerusalem hardly diminished the reality which continnes to extend itself today, that is, the transformation of an insurgent force, fed by the state of emergency in Europe, to an imperial state power, bent on domination of Palestinian life and land. In this regard a starting similarity comes to mind: the quincentennial of Columbus' voyage for the Christian West and the forty-fifth anniversary of Israeli statehood and the twenty-fifth anniversary of the conquest of Jerusalem for the Jewish people. Boldly stated, Israel is the Jewish 1492.[35]

As with the Christian West surveying the 500 years since the voyage of Columbus, Jews have a particular vantage point to analyse the twenty-fifth anniversary of a Jewish-controlled Jerusalem. Has this victory, for example, deepened Jewish

---

35- For Elie Wiesel's celebration of Jerusalem see his "At the Western Wall,"in Irving Abrahamson, ed., *Against Silence: The Voice and Vision of Elie Wiesel,* Vol. 2 (New York: Holocaust Library, 1985), pp.187-188. Also see Abraham Joshua Heschel, *Israel: An Echo of Eternity* (New York: Farrar, Straus and Giroux, 1969). With regard to the victory of Israel in 1967 and the taking of Jerusalem, Heschel writes: "As an individual I discovered that I am a wave in the mysterious movement of Jewish history. Israel is the premise, I am the conclusion. Without that premise I am a fallacy. I had not known how deeply Jewish I was" (199). For a recent militarised version of this celebration see American Israel Public Affairs Committee 1992 Policy Statement released on April 5, 1992 and titled "Jerusalem: The Eternal Capital of Israel."

connection with the land of Israel-Palestine or simply solidified Jewish domination of it? Has this victory strengthened Jewish ethical and religious traditions or placed them in grave danger? Has this victory helped Jews to feel more at home in the world or exaggerated our fear and sense of isolation?

Has our empowerment encouraged a generosity of spirit and culture or militarised Jewish bodies, structures, thought and culture? Has the new pride in Jewishness occasioned by Israel also occasioned a shame regarding our actions? Has Israel, with Jerusalem as its imperial capital, ended Auschwitz for Jews or has it simply drawn new borders around the empire - the imperial Israel with "the borders of Auschwitz" recently described by former Prime Minister Shamir? And could it be that to mobilise Jews to maintain and extend this Jewish state, it is absolutely essential to continue Auschwitz as the Jewish anchor of memory and use it as a blunt instrument against those whom we oppress? That in fact with an imperial Israel, Auschwitz can never end?[36]

Of course, in Jewish discourse the terms "ending Auschwitz" and "imperial Israel" are not allowed, and for this reason "our 1492" can only be dismissed. But what if these connections are, in a deep sense, the only way forward for the Jewish

---
36- For Shamir's comment on the borders of Auschwitz see "Israel Charges Pressure by U.S." (*New York Times*, May 16, 1992, Stanley Cohen, "Talking About Torture in Israel" in Lerner, ed., *Tikkun*, 375-387.

people? What if it is these connections which give us pause, force us to think again and stop before it is too late? What if the announcement of Jewish imperial power fundamentally contradicts our claim to innocence and Israel as redemptive? What if Jewish innocence and redemption comes to be seen as covered with Palestinian blood? Could these understandings prompt Jews to recover the human face and peoplehood of those whom we have displaced? And is it possible to articulate a Jewish theology which recognises this displacement as the fundamental fact of contemporary Jewish history, not simply to be lamented or anguished over but to be redressed as the fundamental challenge of Jewish history? Could it be that the only way to address this fact and challenge is to first reconstitute Palestine in the Jewish imagination so as to proceed to a practical politics of implementing this vision?

Here the question is hardly one of moving back before Israel to a Palestine of the past. Rather it is looking ahead to a Palestine of the future which involves a reintegration of what has been split apart in the context of contemporary history. As with Magnes, the question of Jerusalem remains central. On the one hand, the joint governance of a Jerusalem which is capital to Israel and Palestine could lead eventually to confederation of Israel/Palestine in the present. On the other hand, the refusal of Israel to admit Palestinian Jerusalemites to participate in the "peace process," as well as the refusal to recognise diaspora Palestinians - both of which would signal a recognition of Palestinian peoplehood and thus a past and possibly future Palestine - consigns the Jewish and Palestinian future to an extension of and survival within an imperial Israel. Political leaders in Israel, as well as mainstream and progressive Jewish religious thinkers, recognise quite rightly the significance of such recognition as it proposes a subversive narrative undermining the theological narrative which glosses over empire.

Like other empires, Israel seeks to substitute its narrative -Israel- for the indigenous narrative - Palestine - and more; Israel's hope is to destroy the Jewish and Arab narratives of Palestine so that they cease to exist. At the same time Israel seeks to banish or if possible destroy the Jewish subversive narrative, the inclusive liturgy of destruction and Magnes, understanding of Palestine, for example. Military power is absolutely essential in this task as are its handmaidens, mainstream and progressive Jewish theologians and thinkers who celebrate the victory (not, of course, as empire but as a moral crusade over the forces of evil) and draw the limits of dissenting discourse. Our 1492 again comes to mind as a Constantinian Jewish synthesis comes into being: thought and theology in service to state power. But what happens when power is unmasked and the enterprise is seen for what it is? Yes the empire and its court always feel that the future is theirs, that the dissenting narratives have been consigned to death or at least tamed and managed. However, the unmasking of empire therefore unleashes the most dangerous possibility of all, the renewal and expansion of dissenting narratives. If the dissenting narratives unmask the imperial narrative and coalesce to challenge political power, then it is possible that the foundations of empire and the empire itself may fall.

Rather than relapsing into a pre-empire world long since vanished, the fall of the Israeli empire has the possibility of issuing into a post-empire diversity which combines elements of past and present struggling toward a transformed future. Thus in this case, ending Auschwitz is not the dismantling of Israel and the reinstitution of pre-Israel Palestine as if history had stood still, but the movement beyond pre-Israel Palestine and present day imperial Israel to a Palestine/Israel combining elements of, yet transcending both. Mainstream and progressive thinkers who seek to continue Auschwitz see any discussion of a future beyond an imperial Israel as a war to destroy the Jewish people. Despite the rhetoric, they seek to close off a future beyond empire. But the new Palestine discussed here is less a war than a reconciliation with justice, less a battle than a healing, less a splitting than a re-joining in justice of a history which has been, is now, and will be shared by Jew and Palestinian Arab.

So finally the question is what is it that might bring a Palestine of the future into the contemporary Jewish imagination, a Palestine where Jew and Palestinian Arab realise a mutually empowered destiny? Put another way, what kind of Jewish thought, theological or otherwise, can rescue the witness of the inclusive liturgy of destruction and the vision of Magnes, with all their limitations, into a contemporary, less limited vision of a renewed Palestine? In short, what elements need to be added to incorporate aspects of the Jewish narrative and yet limit Jewish control of that narrative so as to give room for an equal and equally compelling Palestinian Arab narrative?

Here we again enter difficult terrain. The replacement of a Jewish controlled narrative with one of equality with the Palestinian narrative can be a charade when the power of the two communities is completely unbalanced. It can serve to justify the imperial power if it speaks only of limiting its advance in the present, the tendency of most progressive Jewish thinkers. Therefore the equality of the Palestinian narrative spoken of here should not be seen as moving toward a two rights position which solidifies Jewish conquest and allows for a Palestinian state on 10-12% of pre-Israel Palestine. Rather, raising the Palestinian narrative in the Jewish imagination advises us of the Palestinians' prior rights, which Jews transgressed, and the displacement of Palestinians, which Jews caused. The initial and prior Palestinian narrative therefore takes precedence over the European Jewish narrative which, when transported into the Middle East, moves from suffering to domination. Consequently, Jews may claim a state of emergency in Europe as the initial reason for actions in Palestine, thus the need for immigration; they may even claim, as Magnes did, a desire to return to Palestine to found a Jewish national home as a legitimate Jewish hope, but they cannot claim as a matter of right the political and cultural disposition of the Palestinian people and their narrative.

From the perspective of Palestinians the Jewish emergency, the desire for a "national home," are both disasters, and part of the Palestinian catastrophe. In sum, Jewish actions in Palestine were and are wrong vis-a-vis the Palestinian Arab people. This understanding is critical to the renewal of Palestine in the Jewish imagination.[37]

37- In some ways the Jewish Israeli writer A.B. Yehoshua is honest about the inability of Jews to claim a prior right vis-a-vis the Palestinians. See his *Between Right and Right: Israel, Problem or Solution?* (Garden City, New York: Doubleday, 1981). For my response to Yehoshua's argument see Marc H. Ellis, "Jewish Progressives and the Ecumenical Dialogue," *University of Dayton Review* 21 (Summer 1991): 50-54.

For if Jews, with our own situation and desires, come to believe that what we did in Palestine and what we do to Palestinians is wrong, and that the continuation of these policies continue the wrong and even negate the positive aspects of a Jewish cultural, educational and spiritual center that some Jews felt would accrue from the policy of settlement, then the Palestinian and Jewish narratives come together in a different way.

Acknowledging the wrong is not simply stopping where the boundaries are drawn today but, with this new understanding, changing the boundaries - changing the internal and external landscape of Jews in relation to Palestine. It means to redress the wrong, it means reparations for the wrong done to Palestine and to Palestinians, and it means a fundamental solidarity with Palestinians as they seek to return and rebuild their own culture and homeland. This solidarity with the Palestinian people includes and moves beyond the question of Jews repeating what has been done to them and beyond a vision of renewed Jewish life in Palestine; it is to see Jewish life in Palestine as one important aspect of a pluralistic Palestine. It means the recognition that Palestinian narrative and peoplehood is authentic, self-generating, and self-contained with or without a Jewish presence. It means that there was Palestine, not only a pre-Israel Palestine with an increasing Jewish minority, but a

Palestine before Zionism, even bi-national Zionism, and there was still meaning, hope, despair - in short everything that marks a human and communal existence.

Ending Auschwitz

Yet within this argument for a future Palestine in the Jewish imagination, one cannot end without stating the obvious difficulties of achieving this goal. Recent works on Jerusalem, for example Amos Elon's *Jerusalem: City of Mirrors* and Avishai Margalit's essay "The Myth of Jerusalem," as well as the more forceful discussion favouring a Palestinian state on the West Bank and Gaza such as Yehoshafat Harkabi, *Israel's Fateful Hour*, and Mark Heller and Sari Nusseibeh, *No Trumpets, No Drums: A Two State Settlement of the Israeli-Palestinian Conflict,* demonstrate the continuing limitations of the Jewish imagination regarding Palestine rather than portending an expanding one. For example, Margalit's essay argues for joint sovereignty over Jerusalem separated, at least for now, from the "problem of the rest of the territories." Mark Heller reluctantly agrees to a two-state solution, but his tone is almost fascist in its stridency. The question of a unified Palestine, when mentioned, is derided. Heller especially compares unfavourably and in fact fulfills the penetrating prediction that Hannah Arendt offered over forty years ago in her 1948 essay "To Save the Jewish Homeland: There is Still Time," when she predicted that if a Jewish state was established by force, "...The Palestinian Jews would degenerate into one of those small warrior tribes about whose possibilities and importance history has amply informed us since the days of Sparta," and in which she held out, at the last moment, the possibility of a unified Palestine. Margalit and Heller compare unfavourably as well with the contemporary Palestinian educator Muhammed Hallaj, whose recent essay, "The Palestinian Dream: The Democratic Secular State," outlines the benefits to both Jew and Arab in a renewed Palestine.[38]

In the final analysis most Jewish writing conspires against such a vision and even in granting a small, demilitarised, dependent Palestinian state (often with these aspects secured by Israeli military power within the Palestinian territorial borders), the

---

38- Amos Elon, *Jerusalem: City of Mirrors* (Boston : Little Brown, 1989); Avishai Margalit, "The Myth of Jerusalem," *New York Review of Books* 38 (December 19, 1991): 61; Yeshofat Harkabi, *Israel's Fateful Hour (New York : Harper and Row, 1988); Mark Heller and Sari Nusseibeh, No Trumpets, No Drums: A Two-State Settlement of the Israeli-Palestinian Conflict* (New York: Hill and Wang, 1991). Heller fulfils the analysis of Edward Said when Said cites the paradox of Jews arguing and internalising Orientalist positions with the backing of Western and Israeli state power. See Said, *Orientalism*, 306-312. Contrast the above with Hannah Arendt, "To Save the Jewish Homeland : There is Still Time," in Ron Feldman, ed., *Hannah Arendt: The Jew as Pariah* (New York: Grove Press, 1978), 178-192, and Muhammed Halaj, "The Palestinian Dream: The Democratic Secular State," in Rosemary Radford Ruether and Marc H. Ellis, eds., *Beyond Occupation: America Jewish, Christian and Palestinian Voices for Peace* (Boston: Beacon Press, 1990), 222-230.

arguments are endlessly detailed and intricate. Could we say that these intricacies, this necessity to bargain Jewish claims with some recently acknowledged Palestinian claims, this levelling of terrain which is called dialogue, may be too little and too late for the Palestinian people? Could we say that a proposed dialogue by two intelligent and well-meaning Jews, Daniel and Jonathan Boyarin, which begins as follows, may be seen as a bit presumptuous by Palestinians:

> We are, ourselves, fully committed to national liberation for the Palestinian people. This commitment is, moreover, seen by us as a direst continuation of our dedication to our own people in several ways. Pragmatically, there can only be hope for a healthy social future for the Jewish people in a world of peace, and peace demands justice for all of the people of the Middle East. There is more than that, however. In our understanding, insofar as Zionism is a movement of national liberation for the Jewish people, sympathy for other movements of national liberation is concomitant with Zionism. It follows therefore, that activity on behalf of Palestine is a direct consequence of Zionism properly understood.[39]

Edward Said's response to the Boyarins' proposed solidarity is more to the point:

> The Boyarins are also unhappy with the insufficiency of my acknowedgement of Jewish suffering: anti-Semitism, they say, is only a subordinate term in my formulation. This I find staggering in its impropriety. Can they not get it into their heads that as Palestinians, whose total dispossession and daily - I repeat, daily - torture, murder, and mass oppression by "the state of the Jewish people" occurs even as the Boyarins speak, we are not always compelled to think of the former suffering of the Jewish people. Can you imagine the brothers Boyarin standing next to the residents of Beita as their houses were being blown up by the Israeli army, and saying to them, "It would help you to know and remember that the Jews who are now killing you were once cruelly and unfairly killed too." Or consoling the parents of a Palestinian child just shot by an Israeli soldier by saying that the

---

39- Daniel Boyarin and Jonathan Boyarin, "Toward A Dialogue with Edward Said," *Critical Inquiry* 15 (Spring 1989): 627. Jonathan Boyarin's work on the issue of Jewish memory is quite interesting but in the end fails to deal with the urgency of the concrete situation in Israel/Palestine. See his *Storm From Paradise: The Politics of Jewish Memory* (Minneapolis: University of Minnesota Press, 1992).

> soldier may have had relatives who were exterminated by the Nazis. What kind of loony tactlessness is at work here, as if "dialogue" with Palestinians was completely separable from the outrages taking pace in the Occupied Territories?[40]

Said seems to be saying that the primary issue for Palestinians - and by extension for Jews as well at this point in time - is not Jewish history or memory or even solidarity, but the concrete opposition to state power as it is being exercised by Israel. The memory of Auschwitz and the promise of Zionism as articulated by mainstream and progressive Jews has the effect of sidetracking the issue unless it is subordinated to the primary concern of ending the effects of Auschwitz and Zionism on the Palestinian people. Rather than denying that a Jewish narrative exists or even its importance, Said is calling for a fundamental evaluation of how it functions: to promote, protect or acquiesce in Israeli power or to subvert and end it vis-a-vis the Palestinian people. Therefore Said is calling mainstream and progressive

---

40- Edward Said, "Response," *Critical Inquiry* 15 (Spring 1989): 635-636. Said continues: "What they cannot accept is that the Palestinian and Israeli positions are not symmetrical today, and that whatever the horror of Jewish suffering in the past it does not excuse, abrogate, or exonerate the practices of the Jewish state against the Palestinians by the Jewish state: this must be admitted, and not weakened by constantly calling on people to remember Jewish sufferings in the past, admittedly real and horrifying though they are." (636).

The renewal of Palestine in the Jewish imagination

Jewish theology and thought to account.

And well he might. For in exploring the discussion and dissent of Jews, it is important to remember that the inclusive liturgy of destruction, the Wiesel-Hertzberg discussion and the vision of bi-nationalist Zionists have all been overwhelmed by state power in Israel. Thus what we might call the Jewish tradition of dissent has lost every battle with state power in Israel. Only by breaking with that power, by opposing its extension and calling for its retreat, by subordinating the Jewish narrative to the Palestinian narrative, and by speaking and acting publicly to these ends can the possibility of retrieving this dialogue and dissent be seen as important. For only in the new constellation of empowerment can a renewed vision of Palestine flourish. And only then will the arrogance of a declared solidarity take on substance, as a solidarity recognised by the people who struggle to survive a Jewish power which continues Auschwitz for Jew and Palestinian at the close of the twentieth century.

Afterword

Next Year in Jerusalem

The recent agreement between Israel and the Palestinians on mutual recognition and partial withdrawal from Gaza and Jericho can be derided or applauded, depending on the intentions underlying the accord. From the Palestinian side, there can be only one trajectory: the unfolding over the next years of a Palestinian state, comprised of Gaza, the 'West Bank and Jerusalem. The Israeli projection, the controlling one at this time, is distinctly different: the limited self-rule now proposed for Gaza and Jericho, will be expanded over time to a somewhat broader Palestinian self-rule, though still limited by the Israeli military, settlements and economy.

To some, the partial withdrawal of Israeli troops may seem to be a victory for the palestinians. In some ways it is, for Palestinian resistance in Gaza has simply become too much of a burden to the Israeli military and body politic. Yet Palestinian acquiescence to the limited quality of the agreement represents at the same time a defeat. Partial withdrawal may become the norm as the years pass by. Perhaps the Palestinians, beset by internal divisiveness, a breakdown of economic support and institutional infrastructure, as well as the continuing burdens of Israeli occupation policies and brutality, have little choice but to go along, hoping for a breakthrough in later years.

Israel, on the other hand, has had little use for Gaza from the beginning of the occupation in 1967. By jettisoning Gaza, it can trim its losses and concentrate more directly on the expansion of Israeli control in Jerusalem and the West Bank, areas of greater strategic, economic and religious interest than Gaza. At the same time, Israel can be seen as acting generously and forthrightly in the Middle East peace process. Thus Israel forgoes a losing proposition, Gaza and reaps benefits in the ongoing propaganda war in the West. How can Palestinians and their supporters ask for substantive assistance in Britain and America to establish a state when the policy of might and beatings instituted in 1988 by then-Defence Minister Yithzak Rabin, is now replaced by partial withdrawal and limited self-rule, overseen by the very same man, now Prime Minister Rabin? The short attention span of public opinion, coupled with limited knowledge of what has been accomplished by Israel through the occupation and what can continue under the umbrella of partial Withdrawal and limited self rule - that is, the expropriation and ghettoisation of Palestinian land and population - makes this propaganda victory perhaps inevitable for those who seek simple solutions to a complex situation.

So Gaza and Jericho first, yes, but only if next year, Jerusalem. A phased negotiated withdrawal is fine if the intent and the plan includes that which will not only limit the advance, but reverse as far as possible the years of occupation. A shared Jerusalem is central to this process because it could eventually lead to an equality of Israel and Palestine, on the ground and in negotiations. Jerusalem is key to Palestinians because it links those Palestinians in Gaza and the West Bank together in a coherent unit rather than a dispirited and ghettoised dependent local population ruled by a dominant Israeli state. But the sharing of Jerusalem is equally important to the future of Israel and Jewish Israelis. A partial withdrawal can only in an ultimate sense lead to Israeli domination of the area and ensure the continuation of a fortress mentality. Such a withdrawal will not lead to an acceptance and freedom of Jews within the Middle East; thus a tactical victory for Israel may in the long run be a strategic blunder of immense historical importance. A sharing of Jerusalem can lead to the opposite: a real end to the occupation, which may also mean an end to fortress Israel and an acceptance of Israel and Jewish Israelis in the region. Thus a true Palestinian

The renewal of Palestine in the Jewish imagination

victory, a reversal of occupation, ostensibly a defeat for Israel, may be, over time, a victory for Israel, as well.

At this moment, it is difficult to know how this agreement will translate into the daily lives of Israelis and Palestinians. The ceremony in Washington was replete with symbolism and emotion; the dramatic handshake between Chairman Yassir Arafat and Prime Minister Yithzak Rabin, seen around the world, enticed all but the most cynical of observers. Many who have lived through this history, who have commented on it and worked actively to overcome the division between Palestinian and Jew, wondered at that moment if a peaceful and just conclusion of this tragic conflict was truly at hand. Who could not assent to the words of Rabin when he said, "We wish open a new chapter in the sad book of our lives together, a chapter of mutual recognition, of good neighbourliness, of mutual respect, of understanding. We hope to embark on a new era in the history of the Middle East."

Yet as he spoke, an ancient road was being widened and resurfaced, a road that would carry Palestinians, and perhaps Arafar himself, from Jericho to Gaza, but that bypasses Jerusalem. As Robert Fisk commented in *The Independent*, "The PLO leader would be granted just one very distant view of Jerusalem, five miles away, the Dome of the

Rock and the walls just visible through a crack in the hills, close enough to taunt him with its presence, far enough to ensure despair."

For me, at least, watching the ceremony on television in a hotel room in Lexington, Virginia, these five miles were as concrete and symbolic as the historic handshake I watched with tears in my eyes. Had we as Jews come this far in our history of suffering and struggle only to deny those whom we have finally recognized their healing and their destiny? Could we be so close to ending Auschwitz, that is healing the trauma of our displacement by healing the trauma of those whom we have displaced, and choose instead to continue Auschwitz by denying a full, mutual, and interdependent empowerment to the Palestinian people?

Two days after the ceremony, the Jewish New Year began. The rabbis preparing their sermons had an unexpected task: to tell Jews why the people who had been demonized by the Jewish establishment should now be seen as possible partners in peace. The Jewish community had learned to demonize the other and now in a startling development had to be re-educated. Is this not the fate of all orthodoxy, with its triumphal sensibility and certainty of truth, that one day it be humbled by the diversity of life and especially by the face of the other that confronts the victor with blood and tears and even, amazingly, with an outstretched hand?

The renewal of Palestine in the Jewish imagination

This outstretched hand offered by Arafat was, at least to my eyes, trembling with anticipation and a dignity which held forth the possibility of a healing. The time is now for a healing of Jew and Palestinian, a healing of the damage rendered by expropriation, displacement, exile and death. A shared life in a shared land represents the beginning of this healing. If the Jewish return to Jerusalem is a destiny fulfilled in our time, it can only be celebrated when the Palestinians return to Jerusalem as well. Perhaps at that time, Prime Minister Rabin will stretch his hand out to President Arafat. A new, far-reaching agreement will be signed which will bury a tragic past and annunciate a future of equality and cooperation. Then the real celebration will begin. May it be so, next year, in Jerusalem.

www.ingramcontent.com/pod-product-compliance
Lightning Source LLC
Chambersburg PA
CBHW072142160426
43197CB00012B/2211